KINGDOM SECURITY

The Rise of Kingdom Sentinels

Napolina Richardson

Trilogy Christian Publishers
A Wholly Owned Subsidary of Trinity Broadcasting Network
2442 Michelle Drive
Tustin, CA 92780

For information, address Trilogy Christian Publishing
Rights Department, 2442 Michelle Drive, Tustin, Ca 92780.
First Trilogy Christian Publishing hardcover edition May 2018
Trilogy Christian Publishing/ TBN and colophon are trademarks of
Trinity Broadcasting Network.
For information about special discounts for bulk purchases, please
contact Trilogy Christian Publishing.
Manufactured in the United States of America

10 9 8 7 6 5 4 3 2 1
Library of Congress Cataloging-in-Publication Data is available.
ISBN 978-1-64773-352-0
ISBN 978-1-64773-353-7 (ebook)

DEDICATION

To Your glory, O Lord!

Whatever is the first to open the womb among the people of Israel, both of man and of beast, is mine.

— Exodus 13:2

To You, O Lord, do I offer my firstfruits offering. You have opened my womb and deposited the revelation that is written on the pages of this book. That which opens the womb is Yours! The glory is Yours.

This book is dedicated to the body of Christ, a global army of sentinels. Arise and position yourself in your watch station and execute kingdom security!

ENDORSEMENTS

One should realize that any place where valuable assets that affect self, souls, societies, and world systems are stored, must have a strong security system and trained observers who monitor the surroundings and develop preemptive measures to counter infiltration and interruptions by threatening forces. Napolina Richardson has addressed these issues with precision as it concerns the kingdom of God and its earthly commodities.

Especially important is how she addresses the kingdom mandate, kingdom agenda, and kingdom calendar. These are the essential "threefold cord" that we cannot allow to be broken and to fall prey to attacks without offering viable resistance, recovery, and restoration to all that is "kingdom" in the earth. She has excellently outlined the steps that must be taken to ensure that "the thief which cometh not, but to steal, and to destroy…" (John 10:10) is stopped in his tracks! This book will prove to be a valuable nexus in that effort. Well done, Kingdom Sentinel!

Dr. Gordon E. Bradshaw

Author, *I SEE THRONES! Igniting and Increasing Your Influence in the Seven Mountains of Culture*

President, Global Effects Movers &Shakers Network and the Demonstration Nation

Apostle Napolina Richardson is definitely a latter-day voice and an apostolic general. A woman with impeccable wisdom and insight regarding the state of the church during these times!

God is calling the Body of Christ to watchfulness, and this book written by Apostle Napolina will serve as a great resource for the kingdom.

Kingdom security should be the interest of every leader and saint of God in this hour of the church. We must be vigilant and focused as the times grow darker and the coming of Christ draws near.

Apostle Xavier Madison Sr.
Voices of Truth International Ministerial Alliance

Kingdom Security and the Rise of Kingdom Sentinels is a timely, prophetic, and action-oriented kingdom manuscript that sensitizes and equips Christians for the end-time agenda.

Apostle Napolina's message will challenge the Body of Christ to their dominion mandate as kings and priest in rapidly changing times. I strongly recommend this book to every kingdom ambassador who intends to forcefully advance God's agenda on the earth.

Festus Adeyeye D. Min.
Abundant Life Christian Center

Dr. Napolina Richardson unpacks a powerful roadmap for kingdom watchmen in an ever-changing world, calling forth a new generation of sentinel leadership to impact nations.

The author skillfully develops the foundation of true Kingdom Security and interests, discussing the interconnections of God's mandate, timing, the birthing process, and how the power of darkness must be disfranchised. There is a sound enunciated in this writing, making a clarion call for a new breed of change agents to watch, walk in authority, and keep their charge to usher in the kingdom of heaven. And there is divine resonance unwrapping God's wisdom for watchmen based on the author's personal history and relationship with God.

I recommend this book to intercessors, prayer warriors, watchmen, governmental leaders, business owners, and prophetic voices who want to expand their spiritual influence and effectiveness to impact communities and the nations.

Will Meier
Founder of Awakening Destiny Global; president of Coaching for Impact; author of *Leaders for Life*

I recommend this book to those who want to reposition themselves in this rapidly changing world with its systems. The servant of God calls for a generation that will not be self-centered or self-seeking but those who want to advance the kingdom of God by putting God's interest first. This book certainly challenges your status quo.

Archbishop Bernard Nwaka

This book, like its author, is innovative and intelligible; it opens pathways of thought-provoking strategies and enlightenment so readers will understand the value of the kingdom perspective in the lives of the believer. This book will challenge you to arise! This is a fascinating piece of literature penned to guide realizing, practical, yet impactful tool that can be effectively implemented to establish Kingdom Security.

Napolina, an ASTUTE CHRISTIAN THINKER, writes a unique combination of apologetics, kingdom analysis, and social and spiritual commentaries. She provides informational topics that are insightful. The Rise of Kingdom Sentinel is a comprehension of brilliant clarity. My friend makes complex conversations clear, and she did it in a revelatory way. This book is a MUST-READ to challenge you in your culture of religious matters as you know it.

Congratulations, Napolina, for giving us your superbly crafted best work of releasing the heart of God for His people in order that we may continue to evolve into the apex of kingdom living. If you feel lost, absent of being relevant in your understanding and intelligent insistence, this book is for you. Thank you for taking us into a truer and worthier witness in our increasingly secularized world and progressively changing culture in the Body of Christ.

Pastor Clinton House, author and pastor

"Central to Kingdom Security are the persons that are directly responsible for its execution and their specific task. We can refer to them as kingdom agents," writes Apostle Napolina Richardson.

This is a must-read for God's end-time undercover agents. You will be better prepared to withstand the vicissitudes of the time as an agent of God's army by applying some of the timeless prophetic principles that this book teaches. Pay attention!

Dr. Obie Agyeman

Apostle Napolina is filled with the purpose and intense passion for God. Her insight into matters pertaining to the Kingdom of God is remarkable. Her work challenges the Body of Christ to a new mindset of kingdom living.

Kingdom Security and the Rise of Kingdom Sentinels is a book for our time, when rapid changes, beliefs, concepts, and values are challenged. Apostle Napolina gives us a roadmap to help us to understand God's kingdom mandate, kingdom agenda, and calendar for our time.

May you embrace Kingdom Security and the Kingdom Sentinels in your life.

Apostle Edwin Arrindell, Christian Faith Ministries International, St. Maarten

Napolina Richardson in this book effectively enlightens and directs God's people in kingdom purpose and workings. It is most imperative that we realize and know Kingdom Interest and the governmental operations of God's kingdom, thus inciting believers to take their rightful place and purpose.

It is my belief that as you read this book, you will see an intelligent description and function of the Kingdom Interest vs worldly interest. Some things that we have been made to believe that are of interest and value are merely distractions from God's Kingdom Interest.

I pray that all who read this book will come into a full knowledge and stirring of the magnificent works and functions of kingdom ministry. Know—understand—advance—protects! Let the kingdom sentinels arise! Exhibit Kingdom Security!

Apostle Jeanette Petrus, Church of the Holy Spirit, Inc., Kingdom of the Almighty God Edification and Training Center

Kingdom Security and the Rise of Kingdom Sentinels is an in-depth, well-structured manual that can be used in learning institutions and personal or group Bible study, especially for those who want to engage the kingdom in a practical yet knowledgeable way.

The author has put a lot of time and intense study into this book. I therefore highly recommend this book to those who want to do serious kingdom business and take back their dominion.

Apostle Peter Barnes, founder and apostolic overseer of Grace Apostolic Ministries, Intl., senior pastor New Direction Grace Church, South Africa

I believe that the Body of Christ, the ekklesia, has entered a new realm, a spiritual era, in which we must adhere strictly to living and teaching the gospel of the kingdom—the principles [legislation] which govern its citizens.

In these changing times—times of uncertainty—believers must know God intimately. It really is about our personal relationship with God, knowing Him as Father and Daddy (Abba). As we listen intently with our spiritual ears, we can tune in to the frequency of heaven. As we obey the instructions of our heavenly Father, we become knowledgeable of how He operates His kingdom. As a result, we are able to acquire new revelations with understanding of how to apply the wisdom of God.

In short, we learn how to prioritize the interests of the kingdom of heaven, and we become a part of the formidable army of intercession watchmen who provide the security required for God's kingdom to advance in the earth. We become sentinels, soldiers who have surrendered their will to God's will and have been trained properly to discern and comprehend, by the leading of Holy Spirit, every aspect of the kingdom of God which commands them to teach biblical truths as opposed to being politically correct.

Apostle Napolina Richardson is to be commended for her astuteness to discern the changing times and call for true watchmen, intercessors, to arise as sentinels who have been equipped and commissioned as kingdom-level servant leaders to provide Kingdom Security—diplomatic immunity—as the Body of Christ develop its perception of our future with Jesus

Christ as our Headship; as we patiently abide God's timing as compared to our selfish ambitions; and, as we assess our individual roles as citizens of the kingdom of heaven, along with our responsibility to represent God in our actions, we begin to mirror Christ.

As an apostle of Jesus Christ, I highly recommend Kingdom Security and the Rise of Kingdom Sentinels as a "must-read," especially for watchman intercessors, those who have been called as sentinels. Apostle Richardson has written an operational manual that pertains to this season of intercession and its importance as believers establish the culture of heaven on earth. This work is a relevant resource to rally the sentinels to advance God's kingdom in the earth to the reality that earth reflects heaven; and therein lay our Kingdom Security.

Dr. James Brewton, vice president of Intercession & Prophetic Ministry, Kingdom Congressional International Alliance, founder and senior pastor [pastorbrewton@gmail.com]

Community Empowerment Ministries, Inc., Allendale, South Carolina

Community Empowerment Family Worship Ministry, Inc., Claxton, Georgia

Founder and president of the Identity Institute School of Ministry

Author, *From Footmen to Horsemen*, Kingdom House Publishing

The talk of the day is kingdom. The book Kingdom Security and the Rise of Kingdom Sentinels will help persons to differentiate the real thing from the mere talk, like the wheat from the tares. This book clearly lays out what is of God's kingdom and what is not. I highly recommend this book to anyone who wants to be equipped to advance God's kingdom agenda on earth.

Apostle Abraham John, the Kingdom Network, Denver, CO

For decades, the Church wrestled to arrive at a place of understanding of God's kingdom, its governing principles, and how those principles should be applied to our daily lives. I have done in-depth research on the subject matter, hoping to arrive at a place of understanding that would be beneficial to my life, my ministry, and those to whom I relate. After reading the text in this book authored by Apostle Napolina Richardson, I have concluded that God has crystalized the understanding of His servant about matters relative to His kingdom, such as what it is, what the governing principles are, and how those principles should be applied to our daily lives. This text would be a life-changer to those who read it and apply its contents to their lives. It is without hesitation that I highly recommend the author and this labor of love to those seeking to clarify issues regarding God's kingdom.

Dr. Terrence A. Allen, overseer of Ekklesia, Richmond, VA

Napolina has made a strong case for kingdom sentinels, kingdom watchmen, and kingdom agents to take their positions on the wall and in the gates and mountains of culture, and to be vigilant, courageous, and tenacious in defending and guarding the Church and the culture from the encroachment, assault, and onslaught of the enemy.

The kingdom sentinels, watchmen, and agents are part of the larger body of Christ and army of the Lord, and they are a specialized type of intercessor and prophetic seer. They will be equivalent to the scouts and sentries in a military unit or national army, and perhaps even to Navy Seals, in a spiritual sense and dimension. She has sounded a clarion call, and I commend her efforts and recommend her book.

Dr. Bruce Cook, The Courts of Heaven, chairman emeritus, KCIA, VentureAdvisers.com, Inc

Kingdom Security and the Rise of Kingdom Sentinels is one of the most revelatory books about kingdom intercession applicable to today's times...that I have read in a long time.

Dr. Napolina Richardson ties in her skills as a seasoned historian to intricately weave together an amazing contrast of national security versus kingdom security.

The roles of the sentinels (watchmen, the intercessors) are portrayed in a detailed specific manner from conception to birth. Through this book, Apostle Napolina is able to give the beginner and experienced "sentinel" a roadmap in helping them to establish kingdom revelatory strategies for kingdom advancement and victory in the times and seasons which are upon us!

Thank you, my spiritual daughter, Dr. Napolina Richardson, for this wonderful handbook for the body of Christ.

Apostle Dr. Sharon Billins, CEO, Palm Tree International Ministries, global spiritual mother of Zion

If a clear understanding of the twenty-first-century Church is important to you, this book is a must-read. Kingdom Security and the Rise of Kingdom Sentinels unmasks the true purpose for the Church as the Father intended from the beginning of time. The Lord has prepared the author of this masterpiece as a vessel of honor for such a time as this. Dr. Napolina, as a surgeon, cuts through inaccurate mindsets and correctly divides the Word of truth.

This book is a clarion call for a new breed of watchmen to emerge in Christ's kingdom and take their rightful place as intercessors who will stand in the gap for this generation. This literary contribution is a monument to God's Word and a testimony of truth, which comes with my highest recommendation to the earnest student of the ways of the kingdom.

May you increase in knowledge, wisdom, favor, and stature in Christ as you read and study this word of truth. Enjoy!

Dr. Mark E. Kauffman, senior pastor, Jubilee Ministries International, CEO, Christian Chamber of Commerce of Western Pennsylvania

TABLE OF CONTENTS

ACKNOWLEDGEMENTS

First and foremost, I give thanks to the Almighty God for being my source and inspiration and for guiding me with His counsel (Psalm 73:24).

To my husband, Kurt Richardson; my daughters, Shammah and Shaddai; and my son, Kurt Richardson Jr., who understood my struggles during this period of writing but stood with me and cheered me on. Darnel Prince and Kendrick Waakzaam, who were also part of this journey.

There were many days when I felt like doing anything other than writing, but the prayers of these loved ones kept me going. My inner circle intercessors prayed me through; and I thank my global army of intercessors; my ROBWIM family for hearing this message over and over and for standing with me. I could not have done this without you.

To my covering, Apostle Edwin Arrindell and Prophetess Yvette Arrindell, thank you for your wise counsel and prayers. And I thank my CFMI family for your continual support and prayers.

I thank Dr. Mark Kauffman for reviewing this manuscript; Dr. Bruce Cook for his brilliant work in editing; Dr. Terry Allen and Jennifer Allen for providing me with my writer's retreat; Virgilio Brooks of Danencia Development for consultation; Avril York and Brenda Gafford for your encouragement and support. To everyone who encouraged and motivated me during this journey, I say a big thank-you.

Napolina Richardson

FOREWORD

Dr. Napolina is truly a steward of the kingdom of God. A gate-keeper of truth. A relevant voice for our times in this time of crises throughout the globe. God has raised Dr. Napolina Richardson to champion the cause of the kingdom in real time.

Her insight into the true kingdom and its functionality and practicality are truly ahead of its time. The simplistic way that she brings truth to the table opens the eyes of everyone to the truth that will change the world.

She has been raised for this day and time to blow the trumpet of change. This book will give sight to the blind so people will have the chance to see again and understand the kingdom of God. The thing that we need now in this world is true sight. The truth will make you free.

This book is a must-read for any leader in the world who wants next-level living. She is a modern-day forerunner for the kingdom of God.

Amb. Clyde Rivers

On the forefront of the mind of every sovereignty is its security—the ability of that sovereignty to protect its country

21

and its people. Throughout history, attempts to build security included, among others: building walls around city, building fortresses and lookout points, strengthening armed forces, developing strategies for war, and developing weaponry for battle.

As we continue to examine the issue of national security today, we can find even more sophisticated efforts, which combine national policies and protocols. Secret agents are trained at all levels and strategically stationed for security purposes. Issues of foreign affairs are major concerns, and intelligence remains among a country's top priorities as it relates to security. We can only conclude that security is of utmost importance.

This truth of the importance of security holds for civic government as well as for spiritual government. Throughout the Bible, we can find many examples that are indicative of the importance of security. Repeatedly, throughout the Old Testament, the Bible makes mention of the watchman and describes their role and function. Watchmen were consistently positioned at various posts. They were at the gates of the city, on the walls of the city, and in watchtowers. They were also summoned to watch over nations. These were all security efforts.

In the New Testament, Jesus spoke to the disciples concerning watching and praying. The apostle Paul in Ephesians 6:18 also admonished the saints at Ephesus to be watchful. The ministry of the watchman is key to kingdom security.

There is no time in the history of the Church when the kingdom watchman is more needed than today. We are now living in an era when the enemy has unleashed his arsenal of weapons against the Church to kill, to steal, and to destroy. In spite of such a blaring anti-Christ attack on the Church, it seems as if the Church is in a state of deep slumber (Isa. 56:10–11).

Before He died, Jesus spent time in the garden of Gethsemane and gave the instruction to His disciples to watch and pray lest they fall into temptation. Three times the disciples were found slumbering instead of praying, which is where the Church is at today. The Church today seems to be too easily distracted while a satanic agenda is creeping into many areas.

Dr. Napolina, in her book *Kingdom Security and the Rise of the Kingdom Sentinels*, brings a sense of urgency to bear on this threat that the Church and all of humanity is facing. This book could not have come at a better time.

The watchman is the most important vacancy in the body of Christ that is still waiting to be filled. God is seeking out watchmen who understand the security needs of the kingdom and will commit to carry out this task. He seeks watchmen who, like the sons of Issachar, had an understanding of the times and seasons and what to do in those seasons (2 Chron. 12:32). In Ezekiel 22:30, the Bible states, "*And I sought for a man among them, that should make up the edge and stand in the gap before me for the land, that I should not destroy it: but I found none.*"

The edges around our communities and our nations are down. There are gaps, and the anti-Christ Spirit has been creeping in, unleashing ungodly legislation and soliciting covering from governmental and judicial systems.

The kingdom of God is calling on us to make up the edges around our nations. There is a clarion call for gap standers in this hour. There is a great need for watchmen to wake up from their state of slumber. It is my hope that anyone that reads this book will avail themselves to fill this position.

Kingdom Security and the Rise of the Kingdom Sentinels has added new contributions to the discussions and literature on the ministry of the watchman. It is clearly written with much insight and revelation and can be used as an operational manual for every believer who needs to understand their role in Kingdom Security. It is indeed a masterpiece that rightly analyzes current threats to God's kingdom and points out necessary actions to deal with the matter.

Dr. Napolina has skillfully and intelligently communicated the need for us to come to a place of appreciation for the most urgent need of our time, which is the issue of the watchman becoming both strong and positioned.

I appreciate your tireless and dedicated effort in your quest to advance God's kingdom through teachings, writing, seminars, and training regarding sentinel leadership.

I highly recommend this book to be added to your library.

Live long and prosper,

Bishop Kwesi Adutwum
Action City Church New York

1.

——•——

Kingdom Security

And I say unto thee, Thou art Peter, and upon this rock I will build my church; and the gates of hell shall not prevail against it.

Matthew 16:18 kjv

We Are Living in Changing Times

Having spent over twenty years teaching social studies and civics to high school students, I have learned many valuable lessons from my students as I encouraged them to open their minds to assess the past, analyze current trends, and envision what the world according to them could look like in years ahead. I often asked them to consider economic developments, emerging social trends, rapid technological development, and the balance of power in the world. It was always amazing to see and hear the things that they would come up with. Some of the things were glaringly obvious while others sparked great debate and challenged our thinking as to what could be and what it would mean to live in the world that they were envisioning.

The truth is, as we look at economic developments, emerging sociocultural trends, technological advances, and the balance of power, we can agree that what was the norm in previous generations has changed tremendously to what we now know and are experiencing today. And for the next generations, we can anticipate even more changes. We are living in changing times. Some of these changes are occurring very rapidly. Before you can come to term with one change, it seems as if another and yet another is already there as well. Changes are often good and can offer great opportunities to all, whereas on the other hand, those same changes, while being beneficial to some, can have serious ramifications for others. Where there are changes and developments, there must also be assessments to acquire the relevant position and response to every development and change.

The developments that we see today throughout the world are not to be taken for granted by the Body of Christ, as they do have serious implications for the well-being of the church. They can affect the extent to which we are free to carry out our God-given assignments on earth or the extent to which we become restricted or censored. These changes also affect the extent to which God's agenda for earth can be freely expressed. Ultimately, they can also affect and infringe on our religious rights. Therefore, as the Body of Christ, it is important that we take time to study all emerging global developments and sociocultural trends and then assess their implications for the body of Christ.

Changing times call for changing measures and changing responses, as well. Therefore, as the Body of Christ, we must not only study the changes, but we must also examine our position and must be prepared to respond appropriately. We should no longer find ourselves merely reacting to these developments, but we should rather be taking a more proactive position in our responses. Therefore, we must be watchful and analyze both in the natural and spiritual realms. We want to understand what the spiritual triggers and the catalyst behind these developments are. Let us take a moment to examine some of these challenges and their implications for the Body of Christ.

As the Body of Christ, we are challenged to deal with a momentum of ungodly legislation and the rise of pressure groups in support of these legislations, who are demanding their enforcement. Biblical truths are being questioned, and godly values are at stake. School curricula are rapidly changing to accommodate newly revised views on gender and sexuality as we are witnessing a steady move toward a genderless society. The church is faced with a dilemma as we are expected to be politically correct as opposed to being biblically correct. To some extent, there have also been divide among some denominations, on whether the church should become politically correct as opposed to being biblical correct. Bibles and prayers are being removed from the classrooms and public places, while SOGI 123 and other such curricula are being introduced in classrooms. Great effort is made by the powers that be to silence the voice of the church. This is a trend that is only likely to increase in the years to come.

Another point of concern for the church as we look at changing times is the spiritual landscape of today. There have also been glaring changes to the spiritual landscape as occultic practices are increasing and becoming more open as satanic interest is advancing. There is a global mushrooming of satanic churches, scientology, new age, freemasonry, and other such groups.

Also, churches are being burned and Christians persecuted as Muslims are seeking to further their agenda of becoming the number-one religion of the world. As Christians around the world gathered in their various houses of worship on Res-

27

urrection Sunday 2019, the news rang out on national media houses and on social media of the horrific bombing of three churches in Sri Lanka. This was an event that took the lives of hundreds of worshipers who had gone out to observe one of the most sacred Christian celebrations, Resurrection Sunday. What was meant as a day of celebration for many quickly became a day of tragedy and mourning.

The truth is, the bombing in Sri Lanka cannot be deemed as just another coincidence. Christianity has been under attack with seemingly increasing intensity and severity in various parts of the world. Accounts of churches being burnt and Christians being killed in Southeast Asia and the Far East is common. This persecution is also widespread in the Middle East, where Christianity is suppressed and is at risk of being wiped out. Churches are pushed to operate under ground, and many are forced to keep their faith as top secret or else…

Attacks on churches and Christians in Africa has also been on the rise. What were once only isolated cases in Northern Africa have now become well-planned and organized attacks throughout Africa. Reports with accompanying horrific images of the killings of Christians, the burning of churches, and attacks on entire villages where congregations and families are hacked to death is becoming more regular. It is spreading from Northern Africa to East Africa and now even into Central Africa. We are experiencing an anti-Christ movement that has been strategically attempting to increase and to infiltrate into the West. This is also evident through the many terrorist attacks that we are now faced with that are insistently targeting the West. Again, the terrorists are well-trained and well-organized in their approach.

All these changes are global. As we examine these phenomena carefully, we will find that a new world culture is emerging that is directly opposing biblical truths and values. These changes must remain a major concern for the church. We cannot roll over and play dead. We must remember that we are His government on earth, and we have the awesome responsibility to partner with Him so that His will can be done on earth. By virtue of such, we administrate on earth on His behalf. Some of the questions that we must now ask ourselves as we examine our response include:

- Is the church powerless against these developments?

- How does it affect the position and role of the church?

- How can we continue to advance His Kingdom despite these developments?

- What spiritual climate are we leaving behind for future generations?

Changing times call for a change in our response, so that we can thrive and be effective as God's government on earth. It is in examining the response and the position of the Body of Christ to such developments that the study and understanding of Kingdom Security finds its greatest significance.

His Kingdom Interest

As we assess recent developments as it relates to the safety of God's Kingdom, we must also study what we will term in this writing as Kingdom Interest and Kingdom Security. As His government we must allow His Kingdom Interest to be realized on earth. That is why Jesus taught His disciples to pray that His Kingdom come and that His will be done on earth as it is in heaven. This tells us that our sovereign God's desire is for us to cause His will to be expressed on earth as it is in heaven. He has plans for earth that He would like to see come to pass. Emerging trends can hinder or oppose His will from being done on earth. Therefore, we must consistently be analyzing the emerging situations and strategizing our response so that we can always stay ahead of the game, since strategies that were used yesterday may not effectively give answers to today's problems.

In order to fully understand our role as His government on earth, we must first understand His Kingdom and its operation. We are kingdom citizens, His government upon the earth. He has entrusted us to handle His kingdom affairs on the earth. Therefore, we are responsible for His Kingdom Interest to be realized here on earth. God is a reigning King whose reign is established forever. Hence, like every other kingdom, there is a government with protocols that relate to its operation. According to protocol, He will do nothing on earth outside of our invitation to Him, through prayer.

As King, He has ideals for His Kingdom throughout the ages that speak of His Kingdom Interest. We must understand the operation of His kingdom government so that we learn how we are to operate as kingdom citizens and administrate His kingdom affairs on earth. We are tasked in managing His affairs. Therefore, it is imperative that we come into the understanding of the following:

1. The knowledge of His Kingdom Interest;

2. The execution of His Kingdom Interest (we must understand who we are and what our roles are in executing Kingdom Interest on the earth);

3. The advancement of His Kingdom, including:

- Our role in protecting it from anything that would threaten its advancement, and

- How we can enable or facilitate its expansion throughout the earth.

In this light the study of Kingdom Security becomes important. Kingdom Security is important for the execution and protection of Kingdom Interest on earth. It is necessary as the response of the church to every emerging situation that is threatening Kingdom Interest. It positions the church to be watchful and to blow the whistle of impending developments that are threats to God's kingdom interest. In this book, we will be introducing and discussing the concept of Kingdom Interest and Kingdom Security and their relevance in dealing with the changing times.

Kingdom Security Is Comparable to National Security

What, then, is Kingdom Security? Kingdom Security is comparable to national security. Therefore, to understand Kingdom Security, let us first focus our attention on the concept of national security. National security is not a new concept. It has been around for many years and has been the subject of debate among scholars and heads of states. To discuss every aspect of national security would fill an entire book. It is a very wide topic that can vary from country to country; however, its implications are basically the same in every country.

Just as countries have their national interests, so does God's Kingdom have what we can call His Kingdom Interest.

As His government, we must be prepared in our administration to represent and to protect His Kingdom Interest on the earth. We must be prepared to facilitate its prosperity.

For the purpose of this writing, we will examine four tenets of national security, which are also relevant to our understanding of the application of Kingdom Security.

1. Safety and prosperity

National security concerns itself with the safety and prosperity of a country and its citizens. To ensure its welfare and prosperity, every country and sovereignty aims at securing peace and stability within its borders to ensure prosperity. Therefore, they concern themselves with protecting the country against all kinds of national and foreign threats and ensuring that their security is not compromised.

To enhance our understanding of Kingdom Security, let us take what we have just outlined about national security and apply it to Kingdom Security. This calls on us to be positioned to respond to every national or global development in such a manner that it will help to safeguard God's Kingdom Interest. We should not only protect His Kingdom Interest, but we must also facilitate the advancement of His Kingdom on earth in the face of the challenges being brought about by societal changes. Our practice of Kingdom Security calls on us to be:

• **Watchful**

We must be positioned to watch in the natural as well as in the spirit. A proactive approach is necessary. Being proactive calls for us to operate with prophetic dimensions. This means that we must see, hear, or sense a thing before it happens. We must be able to see what is coming and cause any weapons against us to be aborted before it goes into effect. Too often we are reacting after the fact.

Our practice of Kingdom Security should also allow us to intercept, in the spirit, the plans for the ungodly legislation before they are tabled. We must blow the whistle and take precautionary action through prayer and other means. This is the same for the burning of churches. As they are planning these attacks, watching in the Spirit can cause us to become aware of these evil plans and again take the necessary precautionary measures. We must work to become privy of the plans of darkness and thwart such by intercepting their schemes.

- **In prayer and intercession**

As we position to watch, what we see, we must be able to bring to prayer. We must be able to intercede for God's intervention to deal with the matter before the enemy's plans can manifest. Our prayer and intercession must take us into the realms of the spirit to deal with the matter. Jeremiah was set over nations to root out, to pull down, and to destroy but also to plant and to build.

- **Vocal concerning the issues**

33

Being proactive also gives us the opportunity to speak out or to take a necessary position on issues in a timely manner. We must not be caught off guard nor be silenced. We must speak as God's government on earth and represent His Kingdom Interest.

2. Protecting the national interest

As part of their security policies, countries also outline their national interest, which speaks of that which the country has set out to achieve. In national security terms, it is referred to as the national interest. It is a country's goals and ambitions, whether economic, military, or cultural. It allows a country to pursue its national programs.

Our practice of Kingdom Security must make room for Kingdom Interest to prosper on the earth, including what's on the heart of God for any season and that which He intends to bring to pass. We must partner with heaven in giving birth to kingdom intentions for the earth. His kingdom intentions must be protected against satanic interest. We must cause the light of His glory to shine through, even when gross darkness is threatening to cover the earth.

3. Protecting a country's secrets

Very important to national security is the protection of the country's secrets. Countries are careful to protect their strategies and even their military strength and potential. They also seek out to learn the plans and secrets from other countries as means of eliminating any threats to their own security. That is why countries train intelligence agents who are stationed at home and abroad, to detect the plans and strength of the enemy.

These same principles apply in Kingdom Security. There is a great demand for kingdom intelligence. If there is ever a need for kingdom intelligence to be stationed and at work, it is now. Kingdom intelligence is responsible for spying out the plans of darkness and exposing them before they can materialize. Elisha, among many of the other prophets, operated as a member of the kingdom intelligence. In 2 Kings 6, the king of Syria was secretly consulting with his servants to make war against Israel. Elisha as a kingdom intelligence operative intercepted those plans from the spirit realm and communicated them to the king of Israel. The plans of the king of Syria were foiled.

As we are looking at our responses as the Body of Christ to global sociocultural developments and emerging global trends that are contrary to God's Kingdom Interest, like Elisha, kingdom intelligence operatives must cause these evil plans to be exposed from their inception and then foiled.

4. Freedom from foreign influences

As part of national security practices, country guard against other countries controlling or negatively influencing its people or the running of the country. Countries guard against infiltration of foreign ideologies that are directly or indirectly opposed to ideologies that are embraced by that country.

This highlights a startling reality when we assess this in the light of Kingdom Security. Biblical values are being strongly challenged in many ways. Attempts are openly being made to redefine what is a family apart from what God created a family to be. We are living in a time when we are being forced to be politically correct as oppose to biblically correct. We are living in a time, according to Daniel 8:12, where the truth is being thrown to the ground. Isaiah 59:14 also speaks of "judgment is turned away backward, and justice standeth afar off: for truth is fallen in the street" (kjv). We simply cannot roll over and play dead. We must think and consider what spiritual climate we are leaving behind for the next generation. The need for Kingdom Security is great. Kingdom agents must be trained, equipped, and positioned.

When we apply these tenets of national security to the need to safeguard God's interest on earth, it can be termed as Kingdom Security. The concept of Kingdom Security is not new, for it deals with principles and procedures that are already laid out in God's Word. It brings together these principles and procedures about God's kingdom and provides understanding for their application, especially as it relates to dealing with today's issues.

Kingdom Agents

Central to Kingdom Security are the persons who are directly responsible for its execution and their specific task. We can refer to them as kingdom agents. We may be able to identify many groups or tasks, but for the sake of this this writing, we will focus our attention on the following three groups in Kingdom Security.

1. Kingdom intelligence

These agents are all about spying out the plans of darkness, searching out their intentions and making them known. The kingdom intelligence operates with prophetic dimensions. They see and hear in the realms and sound the alarm before an unwanted action can be carried out. They are prophets, secret watchers, seers, hearers, and prophetic intercessors.

2. Special task force agents

These agents are usually assigned special tasks to carry out on behalf of their country. These tasks are often risky and tedious. Even so, in Kingdom Security, we can be assigned certain tasks that art to be carried out either in the natural or through prayer. We must always be available and ready for such assignments as they are important to Kingdom Security.

Nehemiah operated as a special task force agent. As he inquired about God's Kingdom Interest for Jerusalem, he was sent on a special assignment to rebuild the walls around Jerusalem. As kingdom agents, we are key players in Kingdom Security. We must watch to advance His Kingdom on earth. We must be aware of the threats to His Kingdom. We must search out His mind and His Kingdom Interest.

3. Sentinel

A sentinel is a very important role when it comes to kingdom security. Simply put, a sentinel is a soldier who is assigned to look over Kingdom Interest. His assignment can be broken down into four very important tasks.

- **A sentinel is stationed as a guard.** Therefore, he guards and protects the interests of the one that he serves against all forms of intrusion. Any advances must encounter him first. He is positioned to deny access when necessary. As sentinels, we must be positioned to deny access at all times to ungodly legislation.

- **A sentinel watches and challenges all intruders.** The sentinel is alert to his surroundings. He is aware of and watches every possible point of entrance and is positioned to challenge. Therefore, he is an always-ready force to be reckoned with.

- **A sentinel works to prevent surprise attacks.** His approach is always proactive. He has a keen sense of awareness of the activities and developments around him. He meticulously searches them out. He is then able to accurately read into even the slightest movement and anticipate the results. Therefore, he is prepared to foil any surprise attack.

- **A sentinel facilitates kingdom advancements.** His role is key to the prosperity of the kingdom. Once the sentinel is positioned and carries out his task well, it will give the kingdom the space to execute its interest and to thrive.

Studying the role of the sentinel is crucial for our understanding and execution of Kingdom Security. He plays a key role in protecting Kingdom Interest. It serves as an excellent guide as to how we should be executing kingdom security. We must stand guard over kingdom interest on the earth in every season. We must be prepared to protect His interest. In the light of sociocultural developments and global trends, we must be prepared to guard and protect godly values and biblical truths. We must have 20/20 vision in matters relating to God's Kingdom, so that we can foil every satanic intrusion as we partner with God for His Kingdom to advance.

_____ ..... _____

2.

—— ◆ ——

Kingdom Interest

Your kingdom come, Your will be done on earth as it is in heaven.

Matthew 6:10

Kingdom Interest

Having looked at Kingdom Security in the previous chapter, we must now focus our attention on Kingdom Interest. Without Kingdom Interest, there will be no need for Kingdom Security. Kingdom Security is necessary to protect God's Kingdom Interest. The sentinel is a key figure in Kingdom Security and is therefore vital for Kingdom Interest to be realized on earth. In this chapter, we will discuss the following:

- The concept of Kingdom Interest

- The inter-connectivity of Kingdom Mandate, Kingdom Agenda, and Kingdom Calendar as part of God's Kingdom Interest

Matthew 6:10 gives us an important key in understanding Kingdom Interest: "*Your kingdom come, Your will be done on earth as it is in heaven.*" There are two questions that we can ask here: What is it that Jesus really wanted the disciples to understand as He taught them to pray in this manner? Second, what is the desired result that Jesus was pushing them to produce on earth through this prayer? Through this prayer, Jesus was teaching the disciples to come in agreement with heaven for God's Kingdom Interest to be realized on earth.

Let us take some time to further explore the concept of Kingdom Interest. It is best understood when likened to a country's national interest. Every country or sovereignty has a national interest, with clear written policies indicating how their national interest should be handled in terms of internal affairs but also relating to foreign affairs. It speaks of that which a country envisions for its well-being, its growth or development, and its security. We are part of God's Kingdom, therefore it is important that we understand the interest of His Kingdom and our role as kingdom citizens in facilitating the well-being, the growth, and the security of His Kingdom. That is why He taught the disciples to pray that His will be done on earth as it is in heaven. His will speaks of His Kingdom Interest.

Our understanding of Kingdom Interest will help us to understand God's will for earth and our role in the process of His Kingdom Interest being executed on earth. To further understand Kingdom Interest, we will also have to come into the understanding of the Kingdom Mandate, Kingdom Agenda, and

Kingdom Calendar and examine how they are interconnected.

God in His sovereignty has divine ideals for His Kingdom. For His kingdom ideals to be realized, He has given mandates to His created subjects. He further, through His foreknowledge and counsel, devised specific plans through which His kingdom ideals are to be realized. These specific plans are called His Kingdom Agenda. His Kingdom Agenda through His counsel includes His predestined plans for individuals, institutions, localities, businesses, and governments, which are also intended to be carried out within a projected time frame. Let us examine the following chart that will help us to understand Kingdom Interest and how it is intended to be expressed on earth.

Kingdom Interest in the most general sense speaks of the goals and ambitions of God for His Kingdom. It speaks of how God envisions His Kingdom, including His plans to prosper and expand His kingdom. These thoughts concerning His Kingdom are vast and more than our human minds can comprehend. Isaiah 55:9 tells us that His thoughts are higher than our thoughts. Job 11:7 tells us that we cannot fathom the mysteries of God. First Corinthians 2:9 tells us that our hearts cannot conceive the things that God has prepared for us. Job 36:26 tells us that God is great and we cannot understand Him fully. He is simply greater than we can understand.

Kingdom Interest extends beyond religious practices. It is not limited to church-related activities. These goals and ambitions of God's Kingdom can be governmental, economic, cultural, or military. Just as every country or kingdom can speak of their national interest, so it is that the Body of Christ can also speak of Kingdom Interest. God's intention for earth and humanity is His Kingdom Interest.

As we study His Word, we will come to understand that Kingdom Interest concerns itself primarily with His lordship (God's rule and dominion on earth) and the salvation of mankind. His intention has always been to rule the earth through man. From the time that God re-created the earth, He placed Adam and Eve to rule over His creation. The first mandate issued to man was to subdue, to dominate, and to cause to increase the earth that He had just re-created. As such, they were to demonstrate His glory throughout the earth.

The fall of man in the Garden of Eden led to man's loss of dominion to Satan in the earth realm. Through God's plan of redemption, man was rightfully reinstated and positioned to enforce God's government on the earth. However, God's intention for man to dominate and execute His Kingdom Interest never changed. His dominion is everlasting, and His will is established forever. King Nebuchadnezzar made the following statement concerning God's dominion:

For His dominion is an everlasting dominion, and His King-

dom is from generation to generation. All the inhabitants of the earth are reputed as nothing; He does according to His will in the army of heaven and among the inhabitants of the earth. No one can restrain His hand or say to Him, "What have you done?"

—Daniel 4:34–35

The following verses, though not exhaustive, help us to further understand God's Kingdom Interest.

- **God wants to fill the earth with His glory.**

  "For the earth shall be filled with the knowledge of the glory of the Lord, as the waters cover the sea" (Habakkuk 2:14).

- **God wants the light of His glory to push back darkness from the earth.**

  "Arise, shine for your light has come! And the glory of the Lord is risen upon you. For behold the darkness shall cover the earth, and deep darkness the peoples; but the Lord will arise over you and His glory will be seen upon you. The Gentiles shall come to know your light, and kings to the brightness of your rising" (Isaiah 60:1–3).

- **God wants His Kingdom culture utilized and implemented on the earth.**

  "Thy kingdom come, Thy will be done on earth as it is in heaven" (Matthew 6:10 kjv).

- **God wants His children to take territories through evangelization of the lost.**

45

"And this gospel of the kingdom shall be preached in all the world as a witness to all the nations, and then the end will come" (Matthew 24:14).

"And the gospel must first be preached to all the nations" (Mark 13:10).

• **God wants Kingdom dominance on the earth.**

"And the seventh angel sounded; and there were great voices in heaven, saying, The kingdoms of this world have become the kingdoms of our Lord, and of his Christ; and he shall reign forever and ever" (Revelation 11:15).

From a governmental standpoint, Kingdom Interest seeks to establish strong spiritual and physical governance upon the earth. We are His ecclesia (His government) upon the earth. It is through us that He will establish His order. We must aim at allowing His Kingdom Interest to rise and dominate over every other interest.

There is satanic interest that operates through worldly systems and governments to establish its order. Some of the areas in which the church must rise to exert its influence include the seven mountains of culture (family, arts, media, education, government, business, and religion). When the ecclesia does not take its position and dominate in all of these areas, they are left open for satanic interest to dominate.

For too long we have mainly dominated in the religious mountain and have refrained from taking dominion in the other areas, therefore allowing worldly systems to dominate in areas where we were mandated to dominate. As such, these areas have also become safe places for satanic interest to incubate and then oppose God's Kingdom Interest. Satanic agents are positioning themselves on the seven mountains of culture and exerting their influence from top-ranking positions, making it easy for them to facilitate satanic interest on earth.

The challenge against Kingdom Interest is great and continues to increase. We must be watchful and understand matters of His Kingdom and how we as kingdom agents must respond to any threats to His Kingdom Interest.

In one of my seminars on Kingdom Security, I was asked about the role of the church as it relates to end-time prophecies. Indeed, certain things are prophesied in the Bible; therefore their fulfillment is inevitable. Should we just accept those prophecies and go with the flow, or are we still obligated to seek the mind of Christ and pray Spirit-inspired prayers? At all times we must still engage His Kingdom Interest. Second Timothy 3 tells us that perilous times will come. However, even in those times we must continue to engage His Kingdom Interest. We must seek for strategies and wisdom to handle matters in those difficult times.

The international community has been pressing for globalization and a new world order. There are many potential benefits from this; however, we must carefully analyze the full implications from the standpoint of God's Kingdom Interest and Security. We can simply ask this question: Is this in alignment with God's Kingdom Interest, or is it directly or indirectly opposing His Kingdom Interest?

A review of Revelation 13 helps us to understand that there will be a new world order. The prophecies also help us to understand that the anti-Christ will ultimately reign and occupy the seat of government over this "one world order" government. This we can read about in Revelation 13:2, which tells us that thrones, power, and great authority will be given to the anti-Christ to rule over this one world order government. This anti-Christ will serve satanic interest. Revelation 13:7 further states that the anti-Christ is also given authority to make war with the saints and to overcome them.

> *And it was given unto to him to make war with the saints, and to overcome them: and power was given him over all kindreds, and tongues, and nations.*
>
> —Revelation 13:7

The prophecy of Daniel also collaborates with the prophecies of John in the book of Revelation concerning the coming anti-Christ's reign upon the earth and its opposition to God's Kingdom Interest.

> *Thus he said, The fourth beast shall be the fourth kingdom upon earth, which shall be diverse from all kingdoms, and shall devour the whole earth, and shall tread it down and break it in pieces.*
>
> —Revelation 7:23 kjv

End-time prophecies will be fulfilled, but again, the question that we must ask is, what is the role of kingdom agents in representing God's Kingdom Interest here on earth as it relates to the end times? How does the Church execute Kingdom Security in the period leading up to the season when satanic interest will dominate the earth? Or even more importantly, how will the Church execute Kingdom Security during that season?

God has a master plan, and He intends to establish His Kingdom Interest on the earth. In the light of this, He taught His disciples to pray that His Kingdom Interest be realized on earth. Therefore, Kingdom Security must concern itself with understanding, protecting, and defending God's Kingdom Interest even in perilous times. As kingdom agents, we are responsible for causing His Kingdom Interest not only to be established, but also to thrive throughout the earth.

Kingdom Mandate

In order to carry out God's Kingdom Interest on earth, God gave man an authoritative command concerning His creation. This authoritative command is what we refer to as His Kingdom Mandate, which also embodies His intentions and design for man and creation. A mandate, simply put, is an official command or commission to do something. The Merriam-Webster Dictionary gives the following definition of "mandate":

- An authoritative command, especially a formal order from a superior court or official to an inferior one

- An authorization to act given to a representative

So, when we speak of God's mandate, or the Kingdom Mandate, we are referring to God's command to us as it relates to His Kingdom Interest. We cannot understand His Kingdom Mandate separate from His Kingdom Interest.

49

God created man in His own image and likeness and breathed into him the life of God. Like all of us, Adam was a spirit living in a physical body and in a physical environment. As a created being, Adam possessed the DNA of God, which gave him the ability to understand how he was designed to operate as God's steward over all that was created. Adam was designed to operate within the culture of the kingdom in which he was created. He was designed to operate according to the principles and values of God's Kingdom, and so are we. Luke 17: 21 tells us that the Kingdom of God lives within us. Therefore, the life, principles, and values of God's Kingdom are within us, enabling us to live and operate as kingdom citizens.

The original mandate given to man is stated in Genesis 1:26–28 (emphasis mine):

And God said let us make man in our image, after our likeness: and let them have **dominion** *over the fish of the sea, and over the fowl of the air, and over the cattle, and over all the earth, and over every creeping thing that creepeth upon the earth. So God created man in His own image, in the image of God created he him; male and female created he them. And God bless them and said unto them,* **be fruitful, and multiply, and replenish the earth, and subdue it: have dominion** *over the fish of the sea, and over the fowl of the air, and over every living thing that moveth upon the earth.*

In verse 26, God is expressing His mandate for man. God's intention is for man to dominate and rule over His creation. In verse 28, God is giving an authoritative command to man to be fruitful and multiply, to replenish the earth and to subdue it. God expects us to carry out this mandate and to dominate in every aspect in the earth. Again, please note that at no point is this command limited to or referencing only to religious matters. It is a general command meant for every aspect of God's creation as per His Kingdom Interest.

This Kingdom Mandate as given to man is also often referred to as the cultural mandate. In her book *Total Truth*, Nancy Pearcey discusses this mandate and explains why it could be referred to as the "cultural mandate." According to Pearcey, the command to be fruitful speaks of developing the social world, such as building families, churches, schools, government, laws, etc. To subdue the earth means to harness and develop the natural world, including in the areas of agriculture and developing technologies, etc.[1]

Furthermore, the mandate also commands us to fill the earth. We are not restricted or limited to cultural or geographic locations, but we are commanded to go global with this mandate. We must dominate and influence in the broadest sense in the seven mountains of culture (family, education, media, religion, arts and entertainment, government, and finance). The original mandate is absolutely about creating kingdom cultures and building civilizations on earth. We must extend the culture and government of His Kingdom in every aspect of life.

Adam's disobedience in the Garden of Eden cost him his authority to rule and to carry out the original mandate. However, Jesus, through the plan of redemption, came to restore man to his right standing and authority, and He thereby also restored the mandate. This was realized through the Great Commission in Matthew 28:18–20. Jesus, having successfully completed the plan of redemption, restored all authority to the believer:

And Jesus came and spoke to them saying, "All authority has been given unto me in heaven and on the earth. Go therefore and make disciples of nations, baptizing

51

them in the name of the Father, and of the Son and of the Holy
Spirit, teaching them to observe all things that I have com-
manded you; and lo I am with you always, even to the end of
the age (kjv).

⌐/

All believers are made responsible for causing God's Kingdom to
advance throughout the earth and for bringing His kingdom culture
to the nations through the Great Commission. For a long time, the
Church has limited the Great Commission to mere evangelization and
the spreading of the gospel.

The Great Commission is part of God's mandate to His Body,
which in the broadest sense is to be fruitful, to multiply, to subdue,
and to dominate. The Kingdom of God will advance every time the
ecclesia takes its place and establishes dominion in the seven mountains of culture.

We are His government. God does not intend for us to be limited
in any area as we carry out His mandate. Remember, His Kingdom is
within us; therefore, we have His DNA, which represents our ability
to execute things the way He executes things. Genesis 1:26 mentions
the mandate of having dominion over all the earth. Matthew 28:19–20
also speaks of going into all the nations.

The scope of the Kingdom Mandate is global, and not limited. It
calls for a people who would understand that God's Kingdom Interest
is one that is global and that His mandate to the ecclesia is global, as
well. We are to take territories in the seven mountains of culture and
establish His government throughout all the earth. We are His governing people, chosen by Him before the foundations of this world to
advance His Kingdom throughout the earth.

We may struggle to carry out the Kingdom Mandate because perhaps:

- We lack understanding of what Kingdom Interest means.

- We are stuck in religion.

- We are praying but not rising up in dominion and influencing the seven mountains of culture.

- We have become entangled in the affairs of this world and have become distracted.

Kingdom Agenda

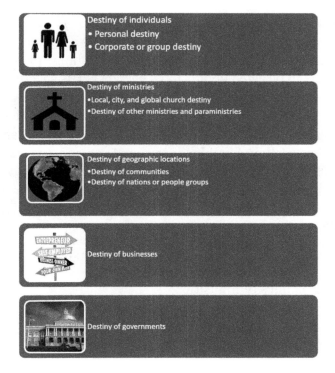

God is a planner. He has plans for our own individual lives, and He has plans for His Kingdom. There are several scriptures that speak of God's plan. Let us look at a few of these.

I know the plans I have for you—good plans to prosper you and not to harm you, to give you a hope and a future (Jeremiah 29:11).

Psalm 33:11 also speaks of His plans: *The counsel of the Lord stands forever. The plans of His heart to all generations.*

Included in His Kingdom Interest are plans for the destiny of individuals, ministries, geographic regions, businesses, governments, etc.

To execute His Kingdom Interest, God has an agenda, which speaks of His more specific plans. An agenda can be considered as a list, a plan, or an outline of things to be done, or matters to be acted upon. God's agenda is His specific plans for the earth and humanity. Therefore, His kingdom agenda consist of plans for individuals, families, communities, nations, and regions throughout the ages. We must collaborate with Him to allow His kingdom agenda to come to pass. To fulfill His agenda, we must position ourselves to carry out our predestined roles on His agenda. We must also pray to make room for His agenda to be fulfilled in the earth realm. We can do so by praying for:

- Understanding of our individual destiny

- Destinies of ministries

- Success of those who are operating in the seven mountains of cultures

- The destinies of nations, families, communities

• Governments

In executing Kingdom Interest, God not only works with an agenda, but also with a calendar. The calendar of God speaks of His divine timing and seasons whereby plans related to His agenda are intended to be executed. Ecclesiastes 3:1 tells us: *To everything there is a season, a time for every purpose under heaven.*

For everything that God has planned and purposed, there is an intended set time for its fulfillment. John Neuhaus III in his book entitled *Melchizedek in Our Midst*, reminds us that "the father orders His work in the earth to mankind according to set times and seasons." He further states that God's plan "is progressively revealed to each generation and to those whom the Father has appointed and chosen and those who are seeking the Lord's kingdom and His righteousness." [2]

When plans on God's agenda become aligned with His calendar for events, it is called the set time of God or the fullness of time. The psalmist, in Psalm 102:13, pointed God to His agenda and reminded Him of His intention to favor Zion and that the set time had come:

*"You will arise and have mercy on Zion; for the time to favor her, yes the **set time** has come"* (emphasis mine). This tells us that time is set. It is predestined before the foundations of the world.

Habakkuk 2:3 also speaks of an appointed time: *"For the vision is yet for an **appointed time**, but at the end it shall speak, and not lie: though it tarry, wait for it; because it will surely come, it will not tarry"* (emphasis mine). Acts 3:21 says, *"He must remain in heaven until the time comes for God to restore everything as He promised long ago through His holy prophets."* These verses make it clear that there is a set time or an appointed time on God's calendar for events on His kingdom agenda to be fulfilled.

Galatians 4:4 also speaks of the fullness of time: "*But when the **fullness of time** was come, God sent forth His Son, made of a woman, made under the law*" (emphasis mine).

Let us take this verse and look at it in the light of Kingdom Interest.

Kingdom Interest was to redeem humanity and to reclaim the Kingdom of God on the earth. On His agenda was the plan of salvation through which His only begotten Son would be sent to earth, born of a virgin. His calendar also stipulated the timing in which this was intended to take place. When there was perfect alignment of what was on His agenda and His calendar, the fullness of time had come.

We must pray at all times for that alignment to take place. The enemy is always at work to bring delays and to cause us to miss divine timing, which will take God's plan off course. Our understanding of God's timing is important so that His kingdom agenda can be executed according to His predestined plans.

The sons of Issachar had great understanding of times and seasons. Daniel also understood God's plan and His season concerning the ending of the desolation of Israel. As a sentinel, he intervened through prayers that triggered a series of events that resulted in God's plan being executed.

Like Daniel and the sons of Issachar, we must have a clear understanding of His Kingdom Interest and the importance of our role in birthing His plans in the earth realm according to His predestined timing.

―――――― ••••• ――――――

3.

———•———

The Believer's Role in Kingdom Interest

For we are His workmanship, created in Christ Jesus for good works, which God prepared before hand that we should walk in them.

Ephesians 2:10

Your Purpose and Kingdom Interest

As we continue to study Kingdom Interest, we will see that we are all created with purpose and that this purpose is linked to Kingdom Interest. Our existence is to facilitate His Kingdom on the earth. It is through humanity that His Kingdom can exercise dominion and increase upon the earth. God expressed His intention for man from the very beginning. This can be seen in Genesis 1:28 (kjv):

And God blessed them, and God said unto them, be fruitful, and multiply, and replenish the earth, and subdue it: and have dominion over the fish of the sea, and over the fowls of the air, and over every living thing that moveth upon the face of the earth.

It is through humanity that God can increase His government and the culture of heaven upon the earth.

Of the increase of His government and peace there will be no end, upon the throne of David and over His kingdom, to order it and establish it with judgement and justice from that time forward, even forever. The zeal of the Lord of hosts will perform this.

—Isaiah 9:7

We are His government on earth. We are in charge of governing and executing His Kingdom Interest on the earth. To clearly understand this awesome responsibility, let us examine the following factors:

We Were Released on Earth with Purpose

Everyone is released on earth through his or her birth to carry out an assignment that is part of God's divine plan for His Kingdom. We often refer to this assignment as our purpose or our destiny. On God's agenda there are specific tasks that He intends to see accomplished at a particular time that are linked to each of us. Our kingdom assignments are time-sensitive. Everyone is released at a specific point in time to carry out a specific assignment.

Therefore, you could not have been born into another time or season. Our lifespan determines the window of opportunity in which we must complete our kingdom assignment. Our assignment should be completed before our eternal transition. We were born with giftings, abilities, strategies, and solutions that are necessary for the success of our assignment.

To further understand our role in Kingdom Interest, we

must focus our attention on the counsel of heaven. This helps us to understand who we are in relation to Kingdom Interest. Robert Henderson, in his book Operating in the Courts of Heaven, outlines a five-step process based on Romans 8:29–30 that helps us to understand the counsel of heaven. These five steps are: foreknowledge, predestined, called, justified, and glorified. [3]

For whom He foreknew, He also predestined to be confirmed to the image of His son, that he might be the first born among many brethren. Moreover whom He predestined, these He also called; whom He called, these He also justified; and whom He justified, these He also glorified.

Let us focus our attention on the first three—foreknowledge, predestined, and called—as we look at our role in Kingdom Interest.

Foreknowledge	Predestined	Called
• Counsel in heaven • Kingdom Interest • God's agenda and calendar	• Counsel of heaven written in books • Destiny of individuals, communities, ministries, nations, and regions	• Released on earth through the birthing process to fulfill that which is written in our books

Foreknowledge

Foreknowledge helps us to understand that God the Father, God the Son, and God the Spirit took counsel in heaven before the foundation of the earth. It is in this counsel that we can find Kingdom Interest. It included God's plans and intentions for individuals, communities, nations, and regions. The following two passages of scripture speak of the counsel of God:

Declaring the end from the beginning, and from ancient times things that are not yet done, saying, "My counsel shall stand, and I will do all My pleasure."

—Isaiah 46:10

For who has stood in the counsel of the Lord, and have perceived and heard His words? Who has marked His words and heard?

—Jeremiah 23:18

Our role in Kingdom Security or in executing Kingdom Interest on the earth is not a decision or a plan that is being undertaken in our lifetime. Neither is it stemming from present national or international developments. Our role was already foreknown through the counsel of heaven. Our omniscient God knows what is needed in His Kingdom at every point in time, and through foreknowledge, He has also decided our role as kingdom agents to secure His Kingdom Interest on the earth. God pointed out to the prophet Jeremiah that his role as a kingdom agent was foreknown—that before he was formed in his mother's womb, he was ordained as a prophet to watch over nations.

Predestined

Predestined speaks of that which is predetermined. We were predestined when the counsel in heaven made the decisions concerning His Kingdom Interest and wrote them down in books. We all have a book written about our role as a kingdom agent. Our books contain the parts of His agenda that are predestined for each of us to carry out. Psalm 139:16 speaks of these books:

Your eyes saw my substance, being yet unformed. And in Your book they were all written, the days fashioned for me, when as yet there were none of them.

Jesus also referred to fulfilling the purpose of God according to what is written in the volume of His book. Hebrews 10:7 states:

Then I said, "Behold I have come in the volume of the book it is written of me—To do Your will, O God."

Called

As we study the calling of Jeremiah, it becomes clear that God knew Jeremiah even before he was formed in his mother's womb. This helps us to understand that we existed in spirit form even before we were released on this earth through the birthing process. In his book *Realms of the Kingdom, Volume Two*, Ian Clayton explains that we came out of eternity with full knowledge of what is written in our book.[4]

He further states that God sets in place and ordains our steps and actions so that we can fulfill an assignment that was already agreed upon before we came to live in this physical realm. We were released on earth with an understanding of Kingdom Interest and with our specific mandate to fulfill our assignment. We were released with great purpose. It is therefore important that we seek every opportunity to understand what we were released on earth to carry out as our kingdom assignment.[5]

Please note that every ability necessary for the success of our kingdom assignment has also been released with us. This includes the giftings and graces that have been placed upon our lives. In 2 Timothy 1:9 Paul states:

Who has saved us and called us with a holy calling, not according to our works, but according to His own purpose and grace which was given to us in Christ Jesus before time began.

We must work on developing our abilities and grace so that we can be successful in our kingdom assignments. We were each released with initiatives and solutions for the time in which we are living.

Working the Bigger Picture

God is a master builder, and therefore He has a master plan for His Kingdom. We all have our individual assignments, but together our individual assignments must complete God's bigger picture and cause His Kingdom Interest and His plans to be birthed in the earth realm.

As I look at how we are to bring all of our individual assignments together to complete His agenda, I am reminded of a jigsaw puzzle. A jigsaw puzzle has many pieces that are meant to complete a picture when each piece is positioned in

its rightful place. God's kingdom agenda can be compared
to that bigger picture, and our individual assignments are the
pieces of the puzzle. Therefore each of us holds a piece of the
puzzle, and we must all bring our pieces together to complete
the picture.

I always enjoyed the challenge of doing jigsaw puzzles. I
remembered starting out with five hundred pieces, but I kept
challenging myself to do even larger puzzles until I was able to
do one thousand–piece puzzles and beyond. As such, I learned
strategies that were necessary to successfully bring the pieces
together to create the bigger picture. Let's look at some of the
lessons that I learned from doing jigsaw puzzles that we can
apply to our assignment and God's kingdom agenda.

- It was impossible to complete a jigsaw puzzle without looking at and studying the picture. As a matter of
  fact, as I was working the puzzle, I needed to have the
  picture in close range and to be constantly looking at
  it to ensure that I was creating that picture. Even so, as
  we are working our assignments, we must continuously seek to understand God's bigger picture, His Kingdom Interest and His timing for its accomplishment.
  We cannot piece it together without continually referencing it. If we fail to reference God's plan, we will
  run into the danger of doing what's in our own hearts,
  what might look popular, what we think it should be,
  or even what we see others doing. By doing so, we can
  cause unnecessary delays and interfere with the completion of the task.

- Each piece of the puzzle is unique and is meant to fit
  into a predetermined place to complete the picture, and
  so is our kingdom assignment. There is no need to try
  to be like someone else. Neither should you be afraid

that someone else will take your assignment from you. There is no duplicate of you. There might be similarities in assignments, but each assignment is unique and is already predetermined. Therefore, we must seek to find our predetermined places and function.

• Each piece of the puzzle is important. Some pieces are meant for the corner, some are designed as end pieces, while others are meant to complete some other part of the picture. However, they are all equally important and necessary to complete the bigger picture. Wherever you are placed to serve in the Body of Christ, be assured that your role is relevant and important in the light of bringing fulfillment to Kingdom Interest. Each of our assignments is necessary and relevant.

• Each piece needs the other pieces to interlock. Our assignments must interlock. We need each other. Our assignments are dependent upon each other; therefore there must also be submission one to the other. We were not designed to operate alone. I believe that even more so in this season, God is raising up teams of like-minded men and women with interlocking assignments to do great exploits. He is raising up and bringing apostolic teams together and sending them forth. We must look for those persons whose assignments are interlocking with ours and embrace them in whatever aspect of ministry they are placed.

• Each piece complements the others. It is amazing that every time you get a piece to fit into its place, how much easier it becomes to fit the other pieces in, as well. We are not to compete with each other in our assignments, but rather we must complement each other. What I am doing with my assignment must facilitate and enhance someone else's assignment. One of the biggest problems that has crept into the Body of Christ is the spirit of competition, where persons are trying to find their own shine and are competing and not complementing each other.

- A puzzle cannot be completed if all of the pieces are not in place. Completion is the ultimate goal. Even so, as God looks at His agenda, His ultimate goal is to see His agenda carried out fully, thus allowing His Kingdom to come on earth as it is in heaven. When we do not rise up to do our part, then we are leaving gaps in the picture, which can lead to delays. Everyone must put their own piece of the puzzle on the table and allow it to interlock with the other predesigned pieces to facilitate its completion. Every piece is important for the completion of the puzzle, regardless of its size or shape.

It is important that we know who we are and understand our role in facilitating Kingdom Interest. His Kingdom must advance on the earth and must thrive over satanic interests. We must rise and create our presence in the seven mountains of culture. In our practice of Kingdom Security, we must maintain our watch over His Kingdom Interest. Our prophetic intercessors must be positioned; our kingdom intelligence and spies must be positioned. Our watchmen must be alert and positioned as sentinels at all times and as special task force agents ready for every assignment.

———————— ••••• ————————

4.

———•———

Opposing Interest

And from the days of John the Baptist until now the kingdom of heaven suffers violence, and the violent take it by force.

Matthew 11:12

A major concern of every country as they seek to execute national security is their foreign policy. In the broadest sense, foreign policy speaks of a country's approach toward other countries to protect its national interest and its citizens. It is to preserve the national security of the country. Foreign policy goals can include the following, among others:

- To maintain the balance of power among nations in order to maintain an environment that is conducive to advancing its own national interests

- Self-interest strategies aimed at safeguarding national interest and achieving a country's goals within its international relationships

- To eradicate all foreign threats to its security

- To know the plans, interest, and strength of other countries and devise policies to strengthen its own national security, being intentional in its approach to any other interest

These principles and concerns of foreign policies help us in our understanding and execution of Kingdom Security. We must also become concerned with the balance of power in the spirit world so that we can cause God's Kingdom to advance and dominate in the earth realm. What we are dealing with in the earth realm are often manifestations of what was conceived in the spirit realm. Our approach toward satanic interest while safeguarding Kingdom Interest must be equivalent to how a country would view and execute its foreign policy.

Bruce Cook, in his book *The Eighth Mountain*, speaks of the two spirit kingdoms and their opposing interests. He states that "there are two spiritual kingdoms—the kingdom of darkness and the kingdom of light, and their respective forces are warring for our souls, our identities, destinies and futures as well as those of every human on planet earth." According to Cook, "this is the basis and cause of spiritual warfare. These kingdoms are in conflict and are diametrically opposed." [6]

We must therefore take our governmental position in safeguarding Kingdom Interest and become intentional in eradicating every satanic threat. As such, we must be fully knowledgeable of satanic interest and its operation so that we will be able to contain it as we strengthen our own Kingdom Security.

As we study Kingdom Security, we must then also focus our attention on satanic interest, the agenda of darkness. We will learn that there is satanic interest that speaks of Satan's goals and ambitions to dominate in the spirit realm and this physical realm. As such, Satan also devises satanic agendas to facilitate his interests. We can easily trace satanic interests back to the fall of Lucifer. Isaiah 14:12–17 helps us to understand the following about satanic interest. It shows us that Lucifer's interest was:

- To be like the Most High

- To have his throne exalted above the stars of God

- To sit on the mountain of the congregation

- To have dominion over kingdoms and systems

- To cause the earth to tremble and revere him

- To destroy cities and geographic regions

- To make the world desolate

As we further study satanic interest, Genesis 4 will help us to understand that the plot of Satan in the Garden of Eden was to gain dominion in the earth and the spirit realm. Even then, he was still pursuing his evil agenda of being the supreme one. Satan wanted dominion over man and all of God's creation.

Kingdom Interest seeks to advance God's Kingdom on earth throughout the ages. Its purpose is for believers to take dominion and execute their kingdom assignments at all times. However, the world of darkness also has its own agenda, which also seeks to dominate and advance against the Kingdom of Light. Their agenda is to spread gross darkness over the earth. Isaiah 60:2 speaks of this agenda of darkness. It states:

For behold the darkness shall cover the earth, and deep darkness the people; but the Lord will rise over you, and His glory will be seen upon you.

As Kingdom agents, we must cause God's Kingdom to advance. We must strengthen our position while we work at eradicating every satanic threat to God's Kingdom Interest. Believers often speak of advancing God's Kingdom. We sometimes also sing about it and truly believe that we are engaging in such activities. But if we were to do a reality check where the balance of power between Kingdom Interest and satanic interest are concerned, we might become alarmed at the rate in which darkness seems to be advancing in areas that are unchecked, taken for granted, or overlooked in our execution of Kingdom Security. We must be proactive and on our watch at all times. Again, I will reiterate that we cannot wait until ungodly legislation is passed and then take action. Our kingdom intelligence and sentinels must detect satanic encroachment and sound the alarm before it is too late.

We are entering a season in which kingdom agents must be aware of every cunning device and strategy of the enemy. We cannot be distracted nor asleep. Kingdom Security dictates that we must be alert, "*lest Satan should take advantage of us, for we are not ignorant of his devices*" (2 Corinthians 2:11).

This does not mean that you must become overly obsessive with satanic interest. If you are not careful, you can find yourself during your time of prayer just dealing with what you perceive to be satanic interferences and not spending enough time dealing with God's Kingdom Interest, thus birthing His interests from the spirit realm to the earth realm. It is important to understand his schemes, devices, and intentions, but you need not to become stuck and preoccupied with such. Rather you must focus on building God's Kingdom on the earth. Therefore, you must operate from the premise of:

1. Knowing your position. You are seated in heavenly places with Christ Jesus, far above principalities and powers and might and dominion, and every name that

is named, not only in this age but also in that which is to come (Ephesians 1:20–21; 2:6).

2. Knowing your authority.

3. Knowing the enemy's position. The enemy is placed under your feet.

To clearly understand the present position of the Body of Christ as it relates to Kingdom Security today, let us do a comparative study of operation of God's Kingdom Interest as opposed to satanic interest in the earth today. We must critically ask the following questions:

1. To what extent is God's Kingdom Interest advancing against satanic interest?

2. What are the present and emerging threats against Kingdom Interest and Kingdom Security?

3. How do we position ourselves as kingdom agents in our practice of Kingdom Security as we examine every emerging threat to Kingdom Interest?

This following list does not claim to be exhaustive, but it serves as a point of reference for this study.

Comparative Study of Kingdom Interest versus Satanic Interest

Kingdom Interest	Satanic Interest
Establish the culture of heaven on earth • Earth must become a mirror reflection of heaven	**Spread the culture of darkness** • Social ills • Systemic injustice and oppressive ideologies • Wars and atrocities
Godly rule over nations • Destiny of communities, nations, and regions • Peace and security	**Anti-Christ rule** • Dictatorship and tyrants • Terrorism • War • Religious and ethnic hatred • Economic and political control
Evangelization of the world • Advancing His Kingdom • Reclaiming lost territories, that the gospel may be preached in four corners of the earth • Healing and deliverance	**Evangelization of the world** • Rapid spread of occultism • Nations closed to Christianity • Terrorism • Burning of churches • Killing Christians
Glory of God to cover the earth • Revival • Church activities	**Darkness to cover the earth** • Occultism • Ungodly legislation
To dominate and transform the seven mountains of culture • Believers to actively participate and dominate in the seven mountains of culture	**To dominate and control the seven mountains of culture** • The spread of darkness through control and dominance in the seven mountains of culture

The Culture of Heaven versus the Culture of Darkness

As we look at the comparative table above, we can see that while Kingdom Interest seeks to promote the culture of heaven on earth, satanic interest is pushing to spread its culture of darkness. It is the intention of God that the earth would become a mirror reflection of heaven, and that His kingdom culture would be expressed on the earth. Therefore, as it is in heaven, so it should be on earth.

As we assess the culture on earth today, we will find that the culture of darkness has been steadily penetrating. Violence, crime, poverty, drugs, and gangs are prevalent in many communities, as well as human trafficking. War, political and economic tensions, animosity, and strife between nations remain dire threats to humanity. Tribalism, as well as ethnic and religious hatred, lead to hostility and genocide as the culture of darkness continues to spread throughout the earth. Satanic interest also spreads its culture of darkness in very subtle ways such as through systemic injustices and oppressive ideologies.

Again, we must assess the extent to which the culture of darkness has been advancing as opposed to the culture of heaven. Our responsibility is to cause God's Kingdom Interest to dominate over satanic interest. Our approach must not only be defensive, but also offensive. We must study the strategies and approaches of the enemy and pray against them. We too often pray after the fact, whereas we should also be discerning the next move of the enemy and taking preventive or pre-emptive action in prayer. As Kingdom Sentinels, we should be alert and vigilant and ahead of the enemy's schemes, causing them to be aborted, unless God allows them. Take a minute to be truthful and ask yourself:

- How often do you pray about world events?

- How often do you pray for God's will to be established in the nations?

- Do you pray against tribalism and racial and ethnic hatred?

73

- Are you creating a world that reflects God's Kingdom and His glory through your prayers?

These are just a few questions that we can use to challenge ourselves or gauge our effectiveness in the practice of Kingdom Security. If we can answer yes to these questions, then we should also ask ourselves:

- How often do we consider these matters in our prayers?

- What percentage of our prayer time is given to these kingdom matters?

We must push back the hand of darkness from the land. We must not give the enemy a free ticket to advance. We must take an authoritative stance to root out and destroy but also to prevent and to contain evil. Remember that Kingdom Security when practiced is most effective when we are proactive, working to prevent and contain satanic interest.

God wants us to pray kingdom prayers. When the disciples asked Jesus to teach them how to pray, He gave them a model of a kingdom prayer. This model prayer is significant to Kingdom Security. We can examine this model from two standpoints: the content or emphasis of the prayer, but also the order and the priority given to the things included in the prayer.

Let us focus our attention on the latter: the order and priority given to the things in the prayer. In this model, priority is given to kingdom matters and that which concerns Kingdom Interest. The model prayer can be broken down into three broad categories, namely:

1. His sovereignty and His greatness ("Our Father in heaven, hallowed be Your name")

2. His Kingdom Interest ("Your kingdom come, Your will

74

be done on earth as it is in heaven")

3. Personal needs ("Give us this day our daily bread and forgive us our trespasses")

This model prayer lays out a protocol for us to use as we approach God in prayer. We often pray the first category and then the third. Some of us might go directly to the third category, bypassing the others. And, there can be a tendency to skip the second category entirely—not because we want to, but rather because we may not connect to it or do not understand how to pray for His Kingdom Interest. Or, we may be too overwhelmed with our personal needs or our worship and adoration of Him.

In this model, praying for Kingdom Interest is placed above praying for our own needs. Remember, Matthew 6:33 emphasizes this as well:

"But seek first the kingdom of God and His righteousness and all these things shall be added to you."

As we approach Him in prayer, we must be compelled to pray that His Kingdom be established on the earth, that His sovereign will be done as it is in heaven, and that His kingdom culture and glory would cover the earth as the waters cover the sea. We can paraphrase that line by saying: "Let your Kingdom Interest be established on earth as You have predestined it and as it is in heaven."

Here is where we pray for the nations. Here is where we seek to know the mind and intentions of God for the earth. Here is where we contend against darkness and satanic interference. It holds great significance in this model and must not be overlooked.

God has the solution for every emerging situation on the face of the earth. It is through engaging His Kingdom Interest in our time of prayer that we will download the relevant responses to deal with every manifesting satanic interest. We may sometimes appear to be blindsided or ill-equipped to deal with the issues when we fall short in the proper execution and application of this model prayer that Jesus has given to us. He knows why He taught the disciples to pray in that manner.

Kingdom Security concerns itself with praying this model on a regular basis. Praying according to this model will facilitate the advancing of His Kingdom and the containment of satanic interest.

The Godly Rule over Nations versus the Rule of Darkness over Nations

God wants to establish His godly rule over the nations of the earth. The seventh angel in Revelation 11:15 sounded the trumpet, and there were great voices in heaven saying, *"The kingdoms of the world are become the kingdoms of our Lord, and of His Christ; and He shall reign forever and ever."*

Kingdom Interest concerns itself with godly rule over the nations. Remember that in the council of heaven, books are written about the destiny of communities, nations, and regions. It is the heart of God to prosper the nations and ensure that peace and security be in their borders. In our practice of Kingdom Security, we must connect with the mind of God and bring ourselves into the knowledge of what is written in the scrolls of heaven concerning the destiny of nations. It is then our responsibility to partner with Him and pray it into existence.

Remember that Daniel understood what was written in the

76

scrolls and that which was prophesied by Jeremiah concerning the ending of the captivity of Israel. Daniel did not take it for granted, but he repented and prayed on behalf of the nation, and in so doing, his prayers brought God's intervention on behalf of the nation of Israel. Like Daniel, Kingdom Security will keep us watching over the nations and contending for what is written in the scrolls of heaven concerning their destiny. We must move beyond our personal prayers to warring over the destiny of nations, so that God's Kingdom will be established in all the earth.

When we fail to contend over the destiny of nations, satanic agendas will cover the earth. Gross darkness will cover the earth, and great darkness will overcome the people if we don't rise up and let the light of God's glory shine through us. Isaiah 14:16–17 tells us that when Lucifer is judged, those who see him will look in amazement and ask:

"Is this the man who made the earth tremble, who shook the kingdoms, who made the world as a wilderness and destroyed cities?"

His evil agenda is to frustrate the plans of God and to spiritually besiege nations and territories. Principalities and territorial spirits are assigned to regions to govern by enforcing ungodly rule and darkness over those territories. The apostle Paul encouraged the church at Ephesus to be prepared to withstand the wiles of the enemy. In Ephesians 6:12, Paul reminded them that:

We do not wrestle against flesh and blood, but against principalities, against powers, against rulers of darkness of this age, against spiritual hosts of wickedness in the heavenly places.

Similarly, in Colossians 1:16 Paul acknowledges the existence of these entities, but he also points out that God has the ultimate authority over them as the Creator:

"For by him all things were created: things in heaven and on earth, visible and invisible, whether thrones or powers or rulers or authorities; all things were created by him and for him" (kjv).

These spirits that are referenced here are governmental spirits that rule over territories. They build strongholds over communities, cities, nations, and territories and enforce ungodliness, holding them bound to their rule. These spirits often enforce dictatorship, tyranny, terrorism, tribalism, war, corruption, poverty, lack, malnutrition, enslavement, and human trafficking over the nations.

It is our job in Kingdom Security to unseat these ruling demonic spirits and cause the glory of God to be experienced in the nations of the world. As kingdom agents, we must enter into the courts of heaven to present cases on behalf of nations, unlocking their destinies. Every demonic stronghold must be brought down, and every principality must be displaced.

Evangelization of the World versus the Expansion of Darkness

In the Great Commission, we are instructed to go throughout the world to evangelize the lost. For centuries, the Church has been busy with this commission. Churches are continuously being built, outreach programs are ongoing, and missionaries are traveling throughout the world preaching the good news of salvation. The continual and rapid development in technology and social media are also making it easier to reach the world with the gospel of salvation.

As much as the Church has made great strides in our evangelistic efforts, we are faced with the reality of the seemingly rapid advances of darkness with the equal intent of claiming souls. Occultism is becoming more blatantly open and is rapidly increasing. The enemy agents are just as aggressive in their evangelistic approach to expand and claim souls. Many groups are surfacing daily. The church of Satan, which started as a small enclosed group, has now mushroomed and is spreading to just about every state in America and even throughout the world. Many intellectuals are turning to new age and scientology, universalism, humanism, agnosticism, and atheism.

What, then, is the position of the Church, or from a standpoint of Kingdom Security, how should the Body of Christ be responding to this emerging dilemma? We cannot bury our heads in the sand and hope that it will go away. Witchcraft has been spreading. The response of many churches or believers toward witchcraft has been to ignore it, as long as it is not directly targeting them. In doing so, this posture has been giving it room to grow and expand. We must never give the enemy the room and ground to strengthen its position. Like Jeremiah, we must always be in our watching position to root out, throw down, and destroy that which is false and opposes God.

The satanic agenda has been strategically using a two-pronged approach in its effort of advancing their dark programs: first, through the spread of occultism or the occult, and second, by restricting our evangelistic efforts. There are nations and regions that, due to strongholds of darkness, remain closed to evangelization of the gospel of Jesus Christ. Large parts of Asia, Southeast Asia, Eastern Europe, northern Africa and the Middle East are not open to the gospel as yet.

Believers are often persecuted there, and churches are being burned. The burning of churches and the intense persecution of Christians are becoming more frequent in some of these territories. People are being terrorized for believing in the gospel of salvation.

Again, let us assess and understand our role in these matters from a standpoint of Kingdom Security. Earlier in this chapter, we spoke of the rationale of foreign policies and their significance to Kingdom Security. We were taught to understand that foreign policy concerns itself with the plans, interest, and strength of the enemy, and to devise approaches, plans, and schemes to strengthen its own national security. Likewise, the enemy is also seeking opportunities to frustrate and destroy our efforts of advancing Kingdom Interest. We must stand guard as sentinels and persist against satanic advances in our execution of Kingdom Security.

We have just examined some of the operations of the enemy against our Kingdom Mandate. It is important that we continue to watch and examine the approaches of darkness in advancing its agenda so that we can strengthen our own position. It is of absolute importance that watchmen or sentinels are continually watching and analyzing developments on the earth in the interest of Kingdom Security. The enemy must not get away unnoticed.

It is in this context that the ministry of the watchman becomes important in detecting the advances of darkness and in eradicating every threat to Kingdom Interest, thus allowing the Church to move forward in its Kingdom Mandate. As watchmen, we must also be proactive in our approach. We are kingdom spies and kingdom intelligence agents who must intercept evil agendas, except when they play into God's hand.

The Glory of God Covering the Earth versus the Darkness Covering the Earth

It is the will of God to fill the earth with His glory, so that all humanity will recognize His greatness and His mighty acts. There is no power greater than His, and none that can contend with Him successfully. He is the beginning and the ending, the All-Existing One, the Everlasting King whose kingdom has no end.

Psalm 19:1–4 (kjv) tells us that the heavens and all of creation testify of His glory. They are an eternal witness of His greatness, glory, wisdom, and majesty:

The heavens declare the glory of God; the skies proclaim the work of his hands. Day after day they pour forth speech; night after night they display knowledge. There is no speech or language where their voice is not heard. Their voice goes out into all the earth, their words to the ends of the world.

Psalm 96 further instructs us to declare His glory among the nations and His wonders among the people. God wants His glory to be made known and to blanket the earth. Habakkuk 2:14 also states in agreement, *"For the earth will be filled with the knowledge of the glory of the Lord as the waters cover the sea."*

One may ask: How do you cause the earth to be filled with the knowledge of the glory of the Lord? It takes place by the *ecclesia* rising up in authority and taking its governmental position and demonstrating the greatness of our God, to whose Kingdom there is no end. The Church must rise up and demonstrate the supernatural power of God over the forces of darkness—not just through our words or our preaching, but also through the demonstration of compelling signs and wonders. We know when God's glory has come to a nation or a region because the forces of darkness will be pushed back, and people will be drawn to the brightness of His glory. Isaiah 60:1–2 tells us:

Arise, shine; for your light has come! And the glory of the Lord is risen upon you. For behold the darkness shall come over the earth, and deep darkness the people; but the Lord will rise over you, and His glory will be seen upon you. The gentiles [nations] shall come to your light, and kings to the brightness of your rising.

We must continue to declare the glory of God over the nations, especially those that are closed to the gospel of salvation, so that they will be drawn to the light of His glory. God desires to bring revival to the Middle East, Asia, China, Russia, and every other area that seems difficult to penetrate.

Someone once asked me: "How can you pray for terrorists who are killing so many innocent persons, waging war and killing Christians?" You may be asking the same question. The truth is that the heart of God is burning for them. It is part of His Kingdom Interest, as well as His divine nature, that all might come to salvation (2 Peter 3:9). The blood of Christ has paid for the redemption of those person. It was a perfect sacrifice. We must continue to pray for revival in those regions and nations that the glory of God will draw them to its brightness.

On the other hand, satanic interest continues to push gross darkness over the nations and over the people. We are living in an Anti-Christ era time when the very foundations of our belief and doctrine are being severely challenged. Prayer has been taken out of our schools, and godly values are being challenged and, to some extent, even compromised. We have also witnessed throughout the world ungodly legislation being signed, which hold serious implications for the Church.

There is a movement of ungodliness that is sweeping across the world. It is operating through the hearts of men, though systems, organizations, institutions, and legal structures. It is targeting reasoning and mindsets and is beckoning for tolerance and acceptance. This is part of what Isaiah is referring to as "gross darkness" that is covering the people.

There is great need for Kingdom Security. Where were the kingdom spies and kingdom intelligence agents when these ungodly legislations were being conceived in the heart of man? Kingdom intelligence must become privy to the information and cause it to be aborted so that it does not even reach our legislative halls.

We have been working the other way around, either primarily or exclusively until now. When such bills enter the legislative halls, then we call for meetings, for prayer chains, for phone calls and email campaigns, and for marches. Kingdom Security in its operation must use every specialized agent necessary to safeguard Kingdom Interest. We must skillfully develop the art of watching in the spirit realm to detect even the slightest movement and intention of the enemy. We must operate with 20/20 vision in the spirit realm. Kingdom spies and kingdom intelligence agents are watchers, and they operate with prophetic insight and ability.

Dominate the Seven Mountains of Culture

When God created man, His original intent for man was to govern His creation. Adam was placed in charge of the daily operation and management of all that God had created on the earth. Part of his responsibility as governor, manager, and steward was the growth and development of that which was created. God used strong words in His instructions to Adam, including "to subdue it and have dominion." This speaks of holding a position of control and influence.

This Kingdom Mandate must be carried out in the world that we live in today. It is the intention of God for us to hold prominent positions and occupy spheres of influence in our society and culture so that we will be able to effect godly change and rule in the nations. Bill Bright, Loren Cunningham, and Francis Schaeffer have identified seven spheres of influence that are necessary to transform the nations. These are: religion, family, education, government, media, arts and entertainment, and business.

Adam's mandate to subdue and take dominion would have placed him in a position of prominence and control in these spheres of influence. These are all part of God's Kingdom Interest. The Church, in its effort to carry out its Kingdom Mandate, has attempted to do so mainly through its activities on the mountain of religion.

Tommi Femrite, in her book *Invading the Seven Mountains with Intercession*, states that: "[T]he religion mountain alone has not been able to transform the world. Every mountain must be inhabited and ruled by the church for it to rise to the position God intends." [7] She further states that "to control cities, regions and nations, we have to control the seven mountains that shape culture."[8] According to this author, "The church has lost its ground. And worse still, it is painfully obvious that ungodly forces are in command." [9]

How can the Church rebuild its influence on the other six mountains of influence? We must pray that those who are called to the marketplace would take their places and rule in their sphere of influence. It is by occupying all spheres of influence that we will be able to transform society, making a greater impact and exerting greater influence on the nations.

To this point we have examined the concept and practice of Kingdom Security and its importance in allowing God's Kingdom Interest to prosper and thrive in the earth realm. We have also discussed our roles as kingdom agents. We have looked at world trends and developments that continue to post threats to the advancement of God's Kingdom in the earth. We cannot continue to use outdated strategies to combat emerging problems. The urgency for Kingdom Security is great, and we must be watchful and alert. There is a great need for sentinels to be skilled and positioned on their watch posts. There is a great need for seers and prophetic intercessors to be trained and positioned on their watch posts. In the next few chapters, we will focus our attention on the ministry of the watchman.

———————— ••••• ————————

5.

———◆———

A Call to Watch

Son of man, I have made you a watchman for the house of Israel; therefore hear a word from My mouth, and give them warning from me.

Ezekiel 3:17

Who Is Called to Watch?

I have heard believers time after time discussing whether or not everyone is called to watch. There has been a notion that not all have been called to intercede and that intercessors are the ones who are called to watch. Therefore, many have concluded that not all are called to watch or that there is no need to be diligent to watch as the intercessors are responsible for that.

I have also heard the question being asked if there is a difference between watching and praying. Many have used these two terms synonymously. As such, many have been praying but not necessarily watching. There is a call for believers to take up their position as kingdom agents rightfully executing Kingdom Security. In this chapter, we will examine the truth in this matter as we look at our call to watch.

The first truth that we need to establish is that we are all called to pray. Praying, simply put, is communication and fellowship with our God. It is our way of downloading the mind of our heavenly Father. Through prayer we can connect with Him and come into the understanding of Kingdom matters. Through prayer we can build our relationship with God and mature in our faith walk. Therefore, prayer is never limited to intercessors. Every believer is commanded to pray, and every believer is also responsible for developing their own prayer life. In fact, we are all instructed to pray without ceasing.

The apostle Paul, in his writings to the Thessalonian church, encouraged them to pray without ceasing (1 Thessalonians 5:17). In Ephesians 6:18, the apostle Paul also encouraged the church at Ephesus to pray always. In this passage, the apostle gave further instructions to pray with all kinds of prayer on all occasions. Throughout the Bible, we can find several instructions for praying with different types of prayer. First Timothy 2:1 states:

Therefore I exhort first of all that supplication, prayers, intercessions and giving of thanks be made for all men.

Here the apostle gave examples of types of prayer that can be made. Suggestions of other types of prayer that can be found in the Bible include:

1. The prayer of faith (James 5:15)

2. The prayer of agreement or corporate prayers (Acts 1:14)

3. The prayer of supplication (Philippians 4:6; Ephesians 6:18)

4. The prayer of thanksgiving (Philippians 4:5)

5. The prayer of intercession (1 Timothy 2:1)

What we can learn here is that we all are called to pray, and that intercession is a type of prayer. Therefore, we all should be interceding. There are times when it is necessary to engage that type of prayer. The prayer of intercession focuses its attention on praying on behalf of another, a family, communities, governing authorities, nations, and regions. The prayer of intercession helps to establish God's Kingdom on earth. To be effective in intercession, we must know the mind of God and pray Kingdom prayers. First Timothy 2:1–4 exhorts us to pray for all men:

Therefore I exhort first of all that supplication, prayer, intercession, and giving of thanks be made for all men, For kings and for all who are in authority, that we may lead a quiet and peaceable life in all godliness and reverence. For this is good and acceptable in the sight of God our Savior, who desires all men to be saved and to come to the knowledge of the truth.

There are also several Scriptures in the Bible where we can find commands to watch and pray. This clearly gives the notion that these two activities are not the same, but they are actions that should be done together. To pray is a command, and to watch is also a command, but they are coupled together. They go as hand in glove. The command to pray is important, and equally so is the command to watch.

While praying speaks of communion and fellowship with God, watching speaks of being alert and sensitive. Our watching in the natural and in the spirit realm will make praying more relevant and effective. They must go together. Prayer is so important that the will of God cannot be released unless there is prayer. His desires cannot be fulfilled unless we pray and pray the Word. When we watch in the Spirit and we see the intentions of God, then we pray until it comes to pass. Prayer gives the Holy Spirit the green light to get to work.

Watching allows us to become aware of:

- God's intentions: We must give birth to these.

- Plots and schemes of the enemy: We must come against these.

- Actions already taken by forces of darkness: We must uproot these.

Jesus made reference to watch and pray a few times in the Bible. In Matthew 26:40–41, the night before His crucifixion, Jesus took His trusted disciples with Him to Gethsemane to pray. He had to deal with His Kingdom assignment on earth. On His return to them, He found them asleep.

Then He came to the disciples and found them sleeping, and said to Peter, "What! Could you not watch with Me one hour? Watch and pray lest you enter into temptation. The spirit indeed is willing, but the flesh is weak."

—Matthew 26:40–41

In Luke 21:6, it is recorded that Jesus used the phrase "watch and pray": "*Watch therefore and pray always that you may be counted worthy to escape all these things that will come to pass, and to stand before the Son of Man.*"

Paul also, in his writing to the church at Ephesus, encouraged his readers to "watch and pray" (Ephesians 6:18). The enemy would like to keep us from understanding our responsibility to watch and pray so that we won't be effective agents within God's Kingdom. Effective praying not only means using all kinds of prayer, but it includes watching as you pray. Watching in this context includes the use of not only vision but of all the senses. As you position yourself to watch, you may be hearing, perceiving, and discerning in the natural as well as in the Spirit. It is absolutely not limited to vision only. It is to come into knowledge through the use of any of the senses. The extent to which we will be effective as we watch depends on the level of our spiritual maturity, our relationship with God, our sensitivity to spiritual matters, and our exercise of the gifts of the Spirit. Every believer must be a watchman and therefore has a role to play in Kingdom Security. Remember that it is the effective and fervent prayer of the righteous that will avail much. The enemy is not afraid of believers who are ineffective in their prayer lives.

First Samuel 13 gives us an account of when the Israelites had weapons but were not allowed to sharpen those weapons. If they needed their weapons to be sharpened, they would have to go to the Philistines to do so. The Philistines determined how sharp their weapons would be. The Philistines did not mind that they had weapons; as long as they were not sharp, they were no threat to the enemy.

The same strategy is used against the believer today. Our enemy does not mind if we pray, as long as we are not sharp and effective. As long as we are not watching and praying, as long as we are not praying Kingdom prayers, we are not a threat to the enemy. The problem today is that many believers are praying, but they have not developed the art and skill of watching.

91

The Watch Stations

A watchman, or a sentinel, is always strategically positioned at a point where he can have the widest perspective of his surroundings. He must be able to see, hear, and sense what is taking place. Therefore, he is often operating from an elevated position. As watchmen, we must also elevate ourselves in prayer. We must ascend to the realms of the spirit, where we can operate from a Kingdom perspective. We must learn how to trade in the realms of the spirit and how to access the courts of heaven. We must ascend to the eighth mountain (Dr. Bruce Cook). From that position, we can hear and see in the spirit realm as we watch over ministries, communities, nations, and economic systems. The Bible gives some examples of places where a watchman is usually stationed.

- **The tower**

    Isaiah 21:5 states, *"Set a watchman in the tower."* The tower speaks of an elevated position. It is an outlook post that gives the watchman great perception and a wide view. From this position, the watchman sees at a distance and can announce what and who is approaching; he can sound the alarm if necessary. This is a prophetic ministry. It sees right into the distance and can announce what is to come.

- **The gate**

The gatekeepers were also watchmen. They guarded what went in and out of the gates.

Mosey and Chinyere Madugba, in their book *Understanding the Ministry of the Apostolic Women,* outlined the importance of gatekeepers and listed five spiritual implications.

These spiritual implications for the gate as discussed in their book are the following.[10] The gate represents:

1. A point of entrance or exit

2. A point of control

3. A place of authority

4. A place where the leaders and elders gather

5. A place where legal matters were handled

As watchmen we must also position ourselves at the gates. It is an awesome responsibility to determine what goes in or out of the gates. It allows us to exercise spiritual surveillance. We are responsible to open and lock gates in our families, our communities, and our nation. Evil and unrighteousness must be locked out. Matthew 18:18 reminds us that *"Whatever you bind on earth will be bound in heaven, and whatever you loose on earth will be loosed in heaven."*

Heaven honors the decisions we make at the gates. Elijah locked the skies and caused no rain, and there was no rain unless by his words. Later on, he unlocked the skies and called for rain, and there was rain. We speak to mountains by faith and command them to be removed. All power has been given unto to us. We have Kingdom authority. The keys are in our hands.

As a gatekeeper, we must become more mindful of Kingdom prayers. His Kingdom come and His will be done. We are responsible for opening the gates and allowing the will of God to enter into the gates. This allows His Kingdom to come, as stated in the Lord's Prayer. In the same vein, anything that does not align itself with God's will or that opposes Kingdom

93

expansion and dominance in the earth must be arrested, quarantined, and locked out.

As intercessors, we must position ourselves at the gate. We must watch over the gates of our lives, over the gates of our communities, our nation, and region. In the most comprehensive sense, we must stand at the gate and watch over Kingdom matters. We watch over the gates of His Kingdom affairs.

- **The wall**

Watchmen were most often placed on the walls of the city as their watch post. The watchmen who stood at the gate decided what entered and left the gate and were responsible for opening and locking the gates. The watchmen in the tower and on the walls had the advantage of seeing distant developments. They announced and warned about what was still to reach the gates.

Their vision was prophetic (they could see and hear ahead of time). Their operations are good examples of Kingdom Security in action.

The operation of the watchman on the wall is proactive and on the offensive. Even so, as Kingdom agents, we must also be proactive. When we position ourselves on the walls, we must be able to prevent evil from reaching anywhere close to the gates. We are too often reactive. When another church is burned or there is a terror attack, then we respond. We must become privy to the intentions of darkness and cause them to be aborted before they can materialize.

- **Over nations**

Whereas watching from the tower, the gate, and the walls

gives a notion of watching from a local standpoint, watching over nations gives a global outlook. The prophet Jeremiah was called to watch over nations and regions. It is also our responsibility to watch over the destiny of nations. We must know the mind and intentions of God over nations and stand watch. Kingdom Security concerns itself with nations and godly dominance over nations. Many believers have not matured to that place yet. Most of their prayers are centered around their personal and family problems or their personal or family affairs.

There must come a time when we become more engaged with Kingdom affairs by watching over nations. When you look at the life of King David as a warrior, in his early years he was engaged in many personal battles. He had to fight for his own survival. As David became king, he no longer was consumed in personal battles. David warred to expand the kingdom and conquer territories. As believers, we must also transition from just fighting personal battles, to watching over nations and taking territories for God's Kingdom. We must make time to know the mind of God over nations and pray to birth His Kingdom intentions over nations. There is a transition that needs to take place. We are His eyes and ears on the earth. He will do nothing on the earth before revealing it to His prophets (the watchmen), according to Amos 3:7.

Task Description

Once we have taken our position as a Kingdom sentinel, we must next understand the rules of engagement. How should I be prepared and equipped to be effectively engaged as a Kingdom agent? As a Kingdom agent, we must be able to operate in the gifts of the Spirit, which include the prophetic gifts, the gift of faith, word of knowledge, discernment of spirits, miracles, and signs and wonders. The operation of the gifts of the Spirit allows us to be more effective on our watch.

This should serve not to exempt anyone from taking up their responsibility as a Kingdom agent. The gifts of the Spirit are not for a select or privileged few. The gifts of the Spirit are for the entire Body of Christ. In fact, the apostle Paul in 1 Corinthians 12:31 encourages us to desire to operate in the gifts of the Spirit. Let us not take these for granted but seek to operate and mature in the gifts of the Spirit so that we can be effective as Kingdom agents. As we examine the Scriptures relating to the watchman, we can find the following task description as listed below. The gifts of the Spirit will assist us as we carry out these tasks.

1. **To see and understand** in the realm of the spirit (Isaiah 21; Habakkuk 2). The watchman must have 20/20 vision in the realm of the spirit, with discerning eyes like eagles that can see afar off. The eyesight of eagles is said to be eight times sharper than human eyes. Watchmen do not have ordinary eyes. They see in the spirit. They see what others won't or don't see. They see in dreams. They see in visions. They see in trances. They see straight through situations. A watchman must be a seer and must understand timing and seasons and then declare what he sees (Isaiah 21:6; Habakkuk 2:1).

2. **To hear and understand** in the realms of the spirit (training your ears to hear). The watchman in Isaiah 21:7 is instructed to listen earnestly with great care. Are we listening in the Spirit? God is always speaking. He wants to make His mind known. We must practice staying tuned in and alert at all times. We must learn to know His voice and be able to differentiate it from

our own voice or the voice of another. The Bible says, *"My sheep know my voice and the voice of a stranger they will not follow"* (John 10:5). The problem is that we often spend more time talking to God than listening for His voice. What we call prayer has become lengthy monologues and not dialogues. So, we usually approach His throne room prepared to talk but not to listen. We must train our ears.

3. **To know and understand** the mind and agenda of God for a season. Daniel 9 tells us that Daniel knew from the books that the season in which God had intended to bring an end to the desolation of Israel as spoken by the prophet Jeremiah, had come. He then set himself to seek God to learn more of His intention on this matter. We must be knowledgeable of God's timing and seasons and then seek Him concerning the matter. Those who seek Him will find Him (Jeremiah 33:3; James 4:8). David said, "Early will I seek Him." Seek to know His mind and intentions daily.

4. **To detect** the plans, schemes, and advances of darkness (2 Kings 6). As the kingdom of darkness seeks to advance in the earth, watchmen must be keen to detect even any subtle movements. We must detect their intentions and their activities. The watchman who is alert must be able to detect advances in the natural as well as in the spiritual realms.

5. **To cause to come to pass**. Isaiah 62:6 speaks of the watchman who stands on the wall and will give God no rest until He establishes Jerusalem. The watchman must remain persistent in their handling of God's Kingdom affairs and remain engaged until God brings it to pass. We must be results-oriented.

6. **To cause something to be averted** (2 Kings 6:8–12). When the king of Syria planned with his trusted men a secret attack on Israel, Elisha the prophet saw this in the spirit and informed the king of Israel about their plans, causing the war to be averted. Elisha, as a Kingdom agent, heard in the spirit and acted on it. Like Elisha, we must have our antennas tuned in to what is happening and take intentional steps to cause the plans of darkness to be averted.

7. **To root up, to pull down and to destroy; to build and to plant** (Jeremiah 1: 10). As God reminded Jeremiah of his appointment as a watchman over nations, He also instructed him how to watch. As he watched, he was to root up, pull down, and destroy. When you are watching over nations, you are watching over governments, systems, etc., that are put in place. You must also root out that which has taken root in your life, family, church, and nation that is not of God. We have to get to the root of the situation and start uprooting. If we cut the branches and fail to deal with the root, it will spring up again.

Roots of unrighteousness are ideologies that are contrary to biblical teachings that sometimes take root in the hearts and minds of people. Remember that a tree only dies from the root. The roots feed the tree and give life. The roots sustain growth. Jeremiah was charged to deal with such.

The watchman is also instructed to pull down. We are to pull down demonic strongholds and any high thing that will seek to exalt itself above the knowledge of God, including satanic and witchcraft altars.

We often deal with rooting out, pulling down, and destroying, but we fall short in carrying through the entire instruction. We must also plant and build. If we are to only root out and pull down, we will create a vacuum. Therefore, we must follow through by rebuilding and planting. When we root out ungodliness from the land, we must immediately plant righteousness in the land. When we root out corruption and evil from the land, we must immediately build strong governments.

8. **To sound the alarm/to warn** (Ezekiel 3:17). The

   watchman sees, hears, and then warns. A warning is a statement or event that indicates a possible or impending danger, problem, or other unpleasant situations. Ezekiel was called as a watchman to bring warnings to Israel. As he sat at the gate and heard the plot to poison the king, Mordecai immediately sent warnings to the king about the matter.

9. **To cause the intentions of God to be known**. The watchman operates in prophetic dimensions. He hears, sees, and senses in the spirit and makes known the mind of God to others.

10. **To announce** (Isaiah 21:8). To "announce" speaks of making something known in a public or formal way for the first time. Prophetic utterances are usually announcements of the sayings or intentions of God. The watchman in Isaiah 21:8 announced what he saw. However, we must be careful in how we handle downloads from God's throne. Some downloads are at times classified and sensitive information and must therefore be treated as such. Not all downloads are meant to be

99

announced. We must know whom to announce to and when to announce, what and when to say, and when not to speak. In such matters we must seek the direction of God.

11. **To declare**. To "declare" speaks of making an official and public proclamation of decision and decrees made in the realms of the spirit. We must know the mind of God and declare it. We can declare the timing and seasons of God.

12. **To decree**. A "decree" speaks of a formal and authoritative order, especially one having the force of law. The watchman stands as a legislator for God's Kingdom. Legislators make laws and pronounce decrees. They are actually Kingdom diplomats and ambassadors. They legislate and make decrees on God's behalf. Watchmen must watch and make decrees.[11]

Job 22:28 states that we shall decree a thing and it shall be established. Heaven acts on our decrees. We have the spiritual authority and legislation to either permit certain situations or stand against them. Remember, life and death lie in the power of your tongue. Whatever you decide to allow into your life, home, church, and nation determines what will happen there. When you are not watchful, you can allow danger to your own life, your homes, the church, and the nation.

13. **To give birth** to Kingdom intentions. When God gives a revelation concerning His intentions on earth—whether concerning a nation, a city, a church, or a person—it is not given to us so we can talk about it or wait to see what God will do about it. God reveals His secrets and intentions to prophets and watchmen so that we can

100

come in agreement with Him in prayer and thereby birth those things into existence.

God said in Amos 3:7 that He will do nothing without revealing it to His prophets. The role of the prophet and the role of the watchman is closely linked.

The major prophets were often called watchmen. Ezekiel was called to watch. Jeremiah was called to watch. So were many others. As was mentioned earlier, the ministry of the watchman is linked to the prophetic. Not all watchmen are prophets, but all prophets should be watchmen.

Elijah understood the intentions of God for the nation of Israel in a season when Baal worship became the order of the day. As a watchman, he brought about the purposes of God. The Bible describes him stooping in the birthing position and crying out for rain. He birthed Kingdom purpose.

God is looking for spiritual wombs in which to conceive and birth His purposes on earth. They must be birthed in the realm of the spirit and pulled down to the physical realm. Our prayers should facilitate the manifestation and performance of that which God wants to see happen on the earth. [12]

14. **To expose and disrupt** secrets of darkness (2 Kings 6:12). The enemy should not be able to plo t and devise his schemes on earth and get off undetected. We must become aware of his cunning devices, disrupt them, and expose them. The enemy cannot be given a free course. Elisha exposed the plans of Syria to the king of Israel and in so doing disrupted his plans. When last have you caused the enemy's plans to be exposed and disrupted? We cannot allow him to have a free course.

101

15. **To pray with apostolic authority**. In our execution of Kingdom Security, we must pray with apostolic authority. Mosy and Chinyere Madugba describes apostolic prayers as authoritative prayers that are prayed by persons that understand who they are and the authority that the believer possesses in Christ Jesus. They make demands on heaven over situations. They are prayers made by sons who know their rights in God, and who can exercise their dominion. Such prayers move heaven and shake earth because they are prayed in accordance with God's will, purpose, and plan over a people, a place, or a thing. Through apostolic prayers, Kingdom Interest can be established in the earth realm. [13]

Apostolic prayers stand in authority over situations in nations, communities, governments, and regions and legislate on God's behalf. These kinds of prayers instruct difficult situations to align themselves with the will of God. What would normally need might and power to be removed, apostolic prayers will command to take place by the Spirit of the living God and cause it to be repositioned (Zechariah 4:7). They will cause prison doors to open. They will subdue nations. They command nature and it responds. Joshua commanded the sun to stand still. Elijah commanded the heaven to hold back the rain, and it was withheld for three years. Apostolic prayers cause shifting and breakthroughs to take place. When apostolic prayers are spoken, signs and wonders manifest.

The Watchman and His Relationship with God

Having looked at the responsibilities and requirements for one to be effective as a Kingdom agent, we can conclude that it is

102

not just a walk in the park. It is expedient that each Kingdom agent takes time to build their relationship with God and mature in their Christian walk. Simply put, it cannot be done out of relationship with God. Here is a simple guide to assist us as we set out to build a meaningful relationship with God.

- We must have such an in-depth relationship with God to know His mind and Kingdom intentions (Psalm 63).

- We must constantly be seeking His face (Psalm 63:1).

- We must delight yourself in His presence (Psalm 63:1).

- We must be a God chaser (Psalm 63:2).

- We must live a lifestyle of worship (Psalm 63:3–5).

- We must live a fasted lifestyle (like Daniel did).

- We must be consecrated and separated unto Him.

When we are not in right standing with Him or our hearts are not pure, it blurs our vision and our hearing. We must be vessels of honor, fit for the Master's use. Our lives must be pure and ready to carry His anointing—ready to be used to demonstrate His power, anointing, and glory.

- We must wait on God and meditate on Him (Psalm 63:6)

——————— ····· ———————

6.

————•————

The Ministry of the Watchmen

I will stand my watch and set myself on the rampart, and watch and see what He will say to me, and what I will answer when I am corrected.

Habakkuk 2:1

In this chapter, we want to look at some qualities that each watchman should possess. When an employer has a vacancy that needs to be filled, they create a job description for that position. The job description helps us to understand what exactly needs to be done, and it also helps to profile the necessary skills and qualities to fill the post. In the previous chapter, we looked in detail at the task description, so we now must look at the qualities that are necessary for the watchman in order to be effective as a kingdom agent. Not only do we want to identify these qualities, but we also to focus our attention on the actions necessary to develop them as we position ourselves in Kingdom Security.

The Watchman Is by Nature:

  1. **Is sensitive** to the realm of the spirit and the natural

surroundings.

Let us look a little closer at the word sensitive. The *Free Dictionary* gives the following definition for sensitive: "Quick to detect or respond to slight changes, signals, or influences. Also, capable of perceiving with the sense or senses."

A watchman cannot be slow. He or she cannot detect problems or a situation after the situation has already occurred. The watchman must be quick to detect. He has trained senses like a detective. Not only must he be quick to detect, but he must also be quick to respond. His sensitivity must be so on point that even slight changes or signals should set off his alarm.

Sensitivity will cause you to read into any development. There are some situations that present themselves as harmless. They may look good on the surface level, but they might have serious spiritual implications.

This definition also speaks of perceiving with the senses. To accurately perceive, one must operate with the gift of discernment. It is important for Kingdom agents to operate with the gift of discernment. The gift of discernment allows you to quickly scan and discern the spiritual climate in your surroundings. It allows you to discern what spirits are operating at any particular time. It helps you to discern actions and intentions. It must discern natural things and spiritual things. Therefore, all kingdom agents must seek after the gift of discernment.

The apostle Paul in 1 Corinthians encourages us to seek out the best gifts of the Spirit. In other words, we must first recognize the need for this gift of the Spirit as a Kingdom agent, and then we must pursue it. We must ask in prayer. We must put it into practice. These qualities can be developed through prayer and practice. We must practice in our study of the spiritual climate in our surroundings. Our sensitivity to the spirit realm is key to understanding what God is doing in this season.

2. **Knows to maneuver/navigate** in the realms of the spirit.

We sometimes enter into the realms of the spirit, but we don't know what we should do there. We must:

- Access the courts of heaven

- Know when to speak and when to listen

- Know when to decree and declare

3. **Is inquisitive** in the spirit and in the natural.

A Kingdom agent must be inquisitive in all spiritual and natural matters. The definition itself of *inquisitive* speaks of being curious, inquiring, prying, and being eager to acquire information. An inquirer does not take things at face value, but always seeks to get behind the truth. Secret agents and spies must be inquisitive. They are always prying. They spy out the enemies' secrets. Even so, Kingdom agents must be inquisitive in the realms of the spirit to intercept and disrupt satanic interests. As Kingdom agents understand their roles and position themselves to inquire in the realms of the spirit, they can become privy to the plans of the terrorist groups that are burning churches and cause such actions to be aborted.

A Kingdom agent is not only inquiring and prying in the enemy's camp, but he is also inquiring of God concerning His Kingdom Interest on earth. Even in our relationship with God, we must develop an inquiring attitude and approach His Word with an inquiring heart. In our prayer time, we must inquire for His mind for our affairs and for Kingdom affairs. We cannot afford for our lives to be led by what seems as natural, but our steps must be Spirit-led and inspired.

When we look at the Bible, we will find many examples of persons who inquired of the Lord. Before David made any decision, it is recorded that he first inquired of the Lord. The same can be said of the prophets and priests. They all inquired of the Lord for directions or for the understanding of dreams and visions that they received.

The Kingdom agent must not only be inquisitive about spiritual matters, but he must also be inquisitive about natural situations and developments. Nehemiah inquired about the status of Jerusalem. As a watchman, when he heard of the state that God's holy city was in, he became burdened about what God wanted him to do. The Spirit led him to fast and to inquire about the mind of God for the restoration of Jerusalem.

When you inquire in the natural, you will also have to follow through by inquiring in the Spirit for God's mind on the matter. Nehemiah further traveled to Jerusalem and inspected the situation for himself, giving oversight to the rebuilding process. Like Nehemiah, as we watch and are moved to action, we must also give spiritual oversight through prayer, travailing and fasting for that which God intends to do or restore within His Kingdom. Our prayers facilitate the birthing of Kingdom purposes. They cause, or at least contribute to, the mobilization of actions and events.

4. Has a watchful attitude.

The inquisitive attitude of the watchman will always keep him watchful. Watchful can be defined as watching or observing someone or something closely; being alert and vigilant. It is the thing that is most common to the Kingdom agent. He is a watchman. He must watch and assess in the natural, and also in the spirit. Let us focus our attention on watching in the natural.

Too often, when it comes to the ministry of the watchman, we focus on watching in the spirit and we overlook ways in which we should also be watching in the natural. When you watch in the natural, you pray and present cases to God based on what you see happening around you in the natural. Here is where we often get the burden to pray about something, because of what we see and hear. This is also necessary for spiritual mapping of homes, communities, nations, and regions.

Hosea 4:6 states that God's people perish because of a lack of knowledge. We are in an electronic age that has led to an information explosion, where vast amounts of information is available at our fingertips. Information is easily accessible through various forms and media. Media has also made it possible that we can have access to information even as it is unfolding.

"Adequate knowledge and information of what is happening around us and around the world is needed for us to pray effectively. Information can stir us up to pray. Knowledge of the will of God concerning a particular situation can stimulate the way you pray about the situation." [14]

Here are some things that we can do to keep ourselves informed as we watch in the natural and pray.

- **Keep up-to-date with the statistics and research**. We must pray with knowledge and burden. Every legal counsel carefully prepares his case before going to court. He makes sure his statistics are accurate to prove his case. Every advocate carefully compiles statistics to defend his cause. Statistics are vital in analyzing the situation. It helps to take an informed stance on any matter. Even so, as we are watching over communities and nations, we must also be knowledgeable of the relevant statistics so that we can pray effectively. Where there is an absence of information, as Kingdom agents we should conduct research so that we can pray accordingly and present our case in the courts of heaven. Research will help us to hold an informed position in prayer as we enter the throne room.

- **Follow developments in all forms of media**. It has become easy to stay abreast with world developments through the media. Information has become instant. At any time we should be able to approach the throne of God with accurate information, seeking His mind on the matter or intervention based on current developments.

110

- **Attend meetings.** This is another way of keeping abreast with what is happening. We are often so busy with spiritual things that we miss opportunities to attend town hall meetings where important issues are discussed that affect our communities. As watchmen, we must be proactive and seize every opportunity to pray before hard decisions are taken that can help to advance ungodly agendas on the earth. It is easier to become privy to that information and to make it a matter of prayer, often causing it to be aborted, than to hear that it was approved and implemented, which makes it more difficult to have the decision reversed.

- **Observe your surroundings**. Take time to observe what is happening around you daily. Observe your neighborhood. Whether it is your workplace or your community, take note of developments and changes that are taking place. Sometimes there are blaring signs right in our surroundings that will indicate the spiritual climate of the area and caution us as Kingdom agents.

Having focused our attention on being watchful in the natural, let us now look at how one can be watchful in the spirit realm as well.

Being Watchful in the Spirit

When you watch in the Spirit, you pray and present cases to God based on what you hear and see in the realms of the spirit. You see and hear from God things that you could not have known otherwise. The Spirit of God can take you in

111

the spirit into regions and nations and allow you to see some things and hear conversations. When we looked at watching in the natural, we spoke among other things of being sensitive, doing research, and observing.

While being watchful in the Spirit, you will need to engage these same qualities. An inquiring attitude is very important. As you enter the realm of the spirit, you are inquiring and searching for the mind of God. You are looking to see what He will show you. You are listening to hear what He wants to express. Your relationship with the Holy Spirit is your divine enabler. God reveals His mysteries and His mind to us through the Holy Spirit.

The apostle Paul tells us in 1 Corinthians 2:10: *"But God has revealed them to us through His Spirit, for the spirit searches all things, yes, the deep things of God. For what man knows the things of a man except the spirit of the man which is in him? Even so no one knows the things of God except the spirit of God. Now we have received, not the spirit of the world, but the Spirit who is from God, that we might know the things which are freely given to us by God."*

The apostle Paul also reminded the church at Rome that the Holy Spirit is the divine enabler. When we do not know what to pray for, it is the Holy Spirit who allows us to access the mind of the Spirit and to pray according to the will of God. Romans 8:26–27 (kjv) tells us:

Likewise the Spirit also helps in our weaknesses. For we do not know what to pray for as we ought, but the Spirit himself makes intercession for us with groaning which cannot be uttered. Now He who searches the heart knows what the mind of the Spirit is, because He makes intercession for the saints according to the mind of God.

We must search out through the Holy Spirit the mind of God for the destiny of communities and nations. We must search out the mind of God for seasons, so that we come into the understanding of God's intentions for any particular season. Then, we must facilitate the birthing process of His will on earth by assisting in unlocking their destinies. This is often a process and takes place in a number of ways, including at times through the courts of heaven.

As we set ourselves to watch in the Spirit, here is what we can do:

- **Wait** before Him to hear and see. Spend quiet time in His presence. We need to do away with distractors and remove distractions in the mind. It is amazing how some persons find it so difficult to bring their minds to rest. Their minds are constantly occupied with issues, problems, etc. We must quiet down not only the body, but the mind and spirit as well, and connect spirit-to-Spirit with the King of Glory. Set aside the time to watch and commit to maintaining that time.

- **Cut back on your extra activities.** One of our biggest distractors is busyness. We can become so busy that we don't even find the time to watch in the Spirit. We don't spend enough time waiting in His presence. We can become busy with all kinds of good work and programs in His Kingdom and miss the opportunity to wait for Him and to hear Him speak.

   Remember Mary and Martha. Mary sat at His feet to hear every word, to learn His heart, to learn of His intentions. Martha was busy serving Him and not positioning herself to hear what was on His heart. Her serving kept her from hearing Him for herself, from

113

getting directions for her life, and from getting directions for Kingdom matters.

When we don't position our lives to hear God for ourselves, we will be receiving what He has said secondhand. Too many of us settle for getting His words secondhand, and we don't quiet down our spirit enough to hear God for ourselves. He is a speaking God. He speaks to His children. He wants us to know His heart, but we must practice waiting on Him and sitting at His feet for instructions. Jesus pointed out to Martha that she was distracted, and that Mary was doing the better thing.

"And she had a sister called Mary, who also sat at Jesus feet and heard His words. But Martha was distracted with much serving, and she approached Him and said, "Do You not care that my sister has left me to serve alone? Therefore tell her to help me.

And Jesus answered and said to her, "Martha, Martha you are worried and troubled about many things. But one thing is needed, and Mary has chosen that good part, which will not be taken away from her."

—Luke 10:39-42

- **Question God about matters.** God often reveals to us in part, sometimes through dreams, or we may just see briefly in a vision, or we may hear just one word. Too often we fall short in seeking more clarity to help us piece together what it is that God is intending for us to know. Keep on asking God for the explanation until you can piece it together. Have conversations with God concerning every bit of detail and seek understanding.

We must not lean on our own understanding, and neither can we afford to misdiagnose what we see, sense, or hear in those moments.

When we read the books of the prophets in the Bible, we can see that they questioned God about what they were seeing. The more we engage with Him, the more He will reveal and the more we will develop in our hearing and seeing in the Spirit. Three basic questions that we need to ask when we are seeking clarity concerning what God is revealing to us are:

a. What do You want me to know about this?

b. What do You want me to do about this?

c. When do You want me to act on this?

- **Set a daily waiting time.** Check your schedule and set a time at which you will commit to daily wait before God to hear His heart. You may even want to decide on a place that you will use daily as that place where you will commit to wait. We sometimes find that there are specific places and times of the day where personally it is easier to hear God speaking. We must find that time and that place and commit to make that our meeting time and place. God and Adam had a time set to meet. In the coolness of the day they met and fellowshipped.

Jesus during His earthly ministry often withdrew from the disciples and the crowd to wait on the Father and to hear about His Kingdom intentions for the earth. Even so, we must also find that time and get before the Lord. The psalmist said in Psalm 130:6: "*My*

115

soul waits for the Lord more than those that watch for the morning."

There is much delight when we find that time and place and fellowship with our God.

5. **Communicate.** Communication is an important quality for the watchman. Every watchman must develop their communication skills as communication is key. We must be able to effectively express to God our matters of concern. On the other hand, as we hear God, we must also be able to accurately express the Kingdom ideas and directives as received during our time of watching.

Remember, as Nehemiah heard the bad report of the state of the walls of Jerusalem. he went before God with the matter. During that time, Nehemiah must have heard from God about His intentions of rebuilding the walls of Jerusalem. He accurately communicated with God and obviously received the right downloads necessary for the Kingdom assignment. When the king inquired about what was bordering him, Nehemiah was able to accurately communicate the following to the king:

- The state of Jerusalem

- His desire to carry out his Kingdom assignment and rebuild the walls of Jerusalem

- The letters granting royal access and safe passage that were needed for him to pass through regions of the empire

- The letters granting him authority and permission to collect building materials that were necessary for the completion of the assignment

116

We must be thorough in our communicating. When Nehemiah went in the throne room of God, he came out of the throne room with all the relevant information. He knew what was necessary for the assignment. Jesus often retreated to communicate with His Father. As He heard from His Father, He communicated back to others. In John 12:49–50, He stated:

"For I have not spoken on My own authority; but the Father who sent Me gave Me a command, what I should say and what I should speak. And I know that His command is everlasting life. Therefore, whatever I speak, just as the Father has told Me, so I speak."

As a skilled communicator, we must also know how to handle sensitive and classified information. We must use wisdom. Some information might not be intended to be shared. We must know when to talk and when not to talk. We must be able to be trusted with Kingdom information. Therefore, a watchman cannot be a talebearer, a slanderer, or given to gossip and confusion.

_____ ..... _____

7.

———◆———

Benchmark for the Kingdom Watchman

I have set watchmen on your walls, O Jerusalem; They shall never hold their peace day or night, you who make mention of the Lord, do not keep silent, and give Him no rest till He establishes; And till He makes Jerusalem a praise in the earth.

Isaiah 62:6–7

I have served on several intercessory teams in several churches and for many years. During this time I read many books on prayer and intercession. I studied the Bible looking for every verse that related to this topic. I learned a lot and felt pretty versed on the topic. My lifestyle became one of intercession and spiritual warfare. I taught spiritual warfare whenever there was an opportunity to do so, pulling on others to rise to this noble call.

During this time, God would speak to me about Kingdom Security, a concept that I was trying to understand as He would stir my spirit and make downloads in parts. I would then try to piece the parts together in my effort to fully understand the concept of Kingdom Security. The bottom line is that I thought that I had it all put together, I was very versed on intercession and warfare, and I was really most effective as a Kingdom warrior.

This was soon to change. The Lord was about to wake me up, show me where I was at, show me where He needed me, and then send me on assignment to wake up, position, and train Kingdom sentinels.

In January 2015, as I was fasting, the Lord woke me up at midnight. This was my usual time of prayer, so I got up and prepared to get into prayer. But this time He said to me, "Take your pen and notepad." I quickly took my Bible, pen, and notepad, and I started to write. It was an encounter that changed my life completely. He asked, "Where are the watchmen in My Kingdom?" He then went on to explain and categorize where the watchmen were at. He pointed out that some were not watching because:

1. They didn't understand who they were, and they did not know how to watch as a Kingdom agent.

2. They were ignorant, blind, and dumb, and were therefore useless as watchmen in His Kingdom in this hour.

3. They were asleep and unaware of their state of slumber.

4. Many were distracted and insensitive to Kingdom Interest.

5. They were pursuing their own agenda as opposed to Kingdom Interest.

Wow! When God is evaluating His agents, you just do not want this kind of report card. This is not a good place to be, especially when you are of the opinion that you are completing your assignment well. As I started to do my own assessment based on what God was pointing out about the Kingdom watchman, I came to realize that as much as I felt I was living a lifestyle of intercession, I was ineffective in some areas and by virtue of such I was missing God's standards that are laid out for the Kingdom watchman. Yes, there are standards laid out in His Word for the Kingdom watchman, and for us to be effective, we must work according to His standards. We must bring ourselves to:

- Understand His standards

- Accept His standards

- Apply His standards per His intentions and not according to our own understanding

We must open our hearts and allow the Holy Spirit to enlighten us according to His Word. Interpretation of standards can be subjective. That is why it is important that we lean not on our own understanding and interpretations of any standard laid down in God's Word. Our interpretation sometimes can be influenced by religious practices and traditions, among many other factors. God wants us to know His standards and to measure up according to His standards. He wants us to place the proper value on them and to align ourselves accordingly. Let us look at some standards more closely as they relate to the watchman.

There are several references throughout the Bible that describe the watchman and that can be used as a benchmark. However, there are two references in the book of Isaiah that talk about the watchman to which God has pointed me as He spoke about the state of the Kingdom watchman. For deeper insight into this matter, we will examine Isaiah 62:6–7 and Isaiah 56:10–11. We will use these two Scriptures as our benchmark. Isaiah 62:6–7 gives a clear description of how a good Kingdom watchman should operate. Isaiah 56:10–11, on the other hand, depicts a scenario that tells us what a Kingdom watchman should not be like.

Let us for a moment conduct a comparative study as we examine these benchmarks. As we do so, conduct your own personal assessment and allow the Holy Spirit to point out to you exactly where you are and what are some of the areas in your life that need some alignment. I pray that the Holy Spirit will help you to understand these standards. More than ever before, there is dire need for Kingdom Security to be in full operation, with each Kingdom agent well positioned and aligned according to their assignment.

Benchmark for the Kingdom Watchman

Figure 2: Comparative study of a good watchman versus a bad watchman

Good watchman	Bad watchman
Isaiah 62:6–7	Isaiah 56:10–11
I have set watchmen on your walls, O Jerusalem; they shall never hold their peace day or night.	*His watchmen are blind, they are all ignorant; they are all dumb dogs, they cannot bark; sleeping, lying down, loving to slumber.*
You who make mention of the LORD, do not keep silent, and give Him no rest until He establishes and till He make Jerusalem a praise in the earth.	*Yes, they are greedy dogs which never have enough. And they are shepherds who cannot understand; they all look to their own way, everyone for his own gain, from his own territory.*
Alert **They are watching day and night.**	**They are Blind**
They are knowledgeable and are reminding Him of His promises.	**They are Ignorant**

122

They are not silent.	They are Dumb dogs
Persistent They are giving Him no rest.	They are Sleeping, lying down, loving to slumber
They are Busy with Kingdom intentions	They are Greedy dogs who are seeking their own initiatives
Understanding of God's timing and season	Having selfish ambitions and lacking Kingdom initiatives

Good Watchmen Are Alert; Bad Watchmen Are Blind

The first requirement is to be alert. A watchman must always be watchful in the spirit as well as in the natural. In Isaiah 62:6 God is saying that He has set watchmen on the walls of Jerusalem and they shall not hold their peace day or night. In Nehemiah 4:9, Nehemiah stated that because of his enemies, he set a watch day and night. These watchmen are special task force agents who are on their assignment day and night.

To watch day and night is not an easy task; it calls for much discipline. You must be sharp and alert. Special task force agents discipline themselves and train their spirits to be alert and engaged day and night. So, even if they are occupied in the natural, their spirits must be trained and disciplined to remain engaged in the spirit realm. This means that their spiritual ears must be in tune and their spiritual eyes searching day and night in the realms of the spirit. This is how one will be able to watch day and night.

Nehemiah 4:13–23 portrays Kingdom Security in operation as Nehemiah is deployed on a kingdom assignment. He is sent to hostile terrain to rebuild the wall. He is faced with consistent opposition that will cause delay or stop the work. He is mocked, accused, and ridiculed, and his authority, his loyalty to the king, and the completion of his assignment are all challenged. In spite of these challenges, Nehemiah as a watchman remained alert. He operated as a commander and a special task force agent. Here are some lessons that we can learn from this special task force agent as we set out to develop our skills as Kingdom agents and operate with utmost alertness.

1. Remain focused

Nehemiah was faced with persistent opposition to his assignment, but he continuously maintained the strength of mind to push through the assignment. He worked with a sense of determination to eradicate any opposition that presented itself. He refused to be deterred from his assignment. He remained focused.

Now it happened when Sanballat, Tobiah, Geshem the Arab, and the rest of our enemies heard that I had rebuilt the wall, and that there were no breaks left in it (though at the time I had not hung the doors in the gates), that Sanballat and Geshem sent to me saying, "Come, let us meet together among the villages in the plain of Ono." But they thought to do me harm. So I sent my messenger to them saying, "I am doing a great work, so that I cannot come down. Why should the work cease while I leave it and go down to you?" But they sent me this message four times, and I answered them in the same manner.

—Nehemiah 6:1–4

2. Set priorities

When we fail to set priorities, we leave ourselves wide open for distractions and confusion. Busyness and distraction are the number-one killers of alertness. Busyness leads to distractions, and distractions hinder our alertness. We must order our daily schedules and activities by setting priorities. Eliminate unnecessary activities. Find easy and smarter ways of getting things done.

As special task force agents, we must give priority to receiving daily instructions from the Holy Spirit concerning our assignments. As we read throughout the book of Nehemiah, we see that his Kingdom assignment remained his priority. He allowed nothing to get in the way of him completing his assignment. In his response to Sanballat and Geshem, he outlined this priority by saying, *"I am doing a great work, so that I cannot come down. Why should the work cease while I leave it and go down to you?"* (Nehemiah 6:3).

3. Multitask

Special task force agents must be able to multitask. This helps us to maintain our alertness in the natural and in the spirit. We must be able to watch and pray but also to work, watch, and pray. Multitasking is the ability to effectively handle more than one task at any given time. Here is where we must train our spirits to remain engaged with the assignment even when we are carrying out other tasks. The assignment should never drop because we are at our jobs, or we are taking care of our homes or conducting any other activities. So, the watchmen in Isaiah 62 were able to watch day and night until God brought fulfillment to His promise toward Jerusalem, until their assignment was fulfilled.

An example of a special task force agent multitasking in executing Kingdom Security can be found in Nehemiah 4:

Those who built on the wall, and those who carried burdens, loaded themselves so that with one hand with they worked at construction, and with the other hand held a weapon.

—Nehemiah 4:17

This meant that they were building, alert and watching, but also ready to swiftly move to warfare if necessary. Special task force agents must be able to multitask. Our spirits must continue to engage the assignment even when in the natural we are handling other tasks. Our spirits must be ready at all times to swiftly move into combat even when we are handling other tasks in the natural.

4. Strategize and organize

Watching day and night calls for a high level of strategizing and organizing. Family matters, ministry-related matters, business-related matters, and work-related matters will all need to be organized to facilitate watching day and night. Remember, our goal is to continuously be watchful regardless of whether it is day or night, to carry out our assignments. As we organize, we will also have to strategize to reach our goals. Nehemiah strategically placed groups at various points. He also had them working in shifts. He had the men and their servants to stay in Jerusalem so that they would work at day and watch at night (Nehemiah 5:22).

5. Collaborate

God is globally raising up teams and sending them out on Kingdom assignment. These are men and women who understand Kingdom Interest and are ready to collaborate on Kingdom assignments, men and women who understand Kingdom Security and are ready to rise as Kingdom sentinels in collaborative efforts.

Nehemiah positioned the servants, the leaders, the laborers, the nobles, the rulers, and the trumpeters, and they all collectively worked to ensure that the assignment was completed in the face of fierce opposition. No one person or individual can shoulder the weight of God's mandate in Kingdom Security alone. No one person can shoulder the responsibility of watching day and night in Kingdom Security by themselves. God is bringing together people with various giftings, abilities, authority, and expertise to work together to carry out His mandate for this hour.

So it was, from that time on, that half of my servants worked at construction, while the other half held spears, the shields, the bows, and wore armor; and the leaders were behind the house of Judah. Those who built on the wall, and those who carried burdens, laded themselves so that with one hand they worked at construction, and with the other hand held a weapon. Every one of the builders had their sword girded at his side as he built. And the one who sounded the trumpet was beside me.

—Nehemiah 4:16–18

6. Sacrifice

Watching day and night requires discipline and sacrifice. What is widely missing in the Body of Christ today is discipline—discipline to totally submit and yield to God's Kingdom Agenda. In Kingdom Security, we must be sold out to our assignment of advancing Kingdom Interest as we push back the satanic agenda. This will take us out of our comfort zones.

Your assignment might call for you to intercede and carry out warfare at hours when you might prefer to sleep or be doing something else. At times, it might demand more times of separation in seeking out matters of the Kingdom. It required great sacrifice from Nehemiah and his team as they watched day and night over their Kingdom assignment. They gave up the comfort of their families as they positioned themselves as special task force agents. They were moved out of their comfort zones.

At that time I also said to the people "Let each man and his servants stay at night in Jerusalem, that they might be guard by night and a working party by day" So neither I, my brethren, my servants, nor the men of the guard who followed me took off our clothes, except that everyone took them off for washing.

—Nehemiah 4:22–23

As we look at our benchmark, we found that a good watchman is alert and watches day and night. In contrast, as we compare the watchman described in Isaiah 56, we find that they are blind. The question that comes to mind is: What good is a watchman who is blind? How can a watchman be blind? Many believers find themselves right here. They are praying on their assignment, but they are spiritually blind. The inability to see in the realms of the spirit is termed as "spiritual blindness." A watchman must be able to see in the realms of the spirit. A watchman must also be able to understand what he or she sees.

As we continue to look into spiritual blindness, we will come to understand that it is also the inability to interpret blaring signs and signals. Again, what is the point of seeing signs but remaining clueless as to their implications? A bad watchman is blind to the spiritual implications of natural occurrences as well. There are certain things that take place in the natural but have serious spiritual implications.

Also, some things are seemingly natural occurrences, but their root causes are spiritual. A watchman must be able see straight through such occurrences and discern their implications. If not, then that watchman is blind and will be ineffective as a Kingdom agent. Blindness in this context can also mean that they are not watchful, nor inquisitive. Kingdom Security demands alertness and agents who are watching day and night.

Good Watchmen Reminds God of His Promises; Bad Watchmen Are Ignorant

As I was discussing this topic once, this question was posed to me: "What should we be looking for?" An understanding of Kingdom Security helps us to understand what we should be looking for: knowing and understanding God's mind and intentions for His Kingdom on earth. We watch to make sure that His Kingdom is secure from foreign intrusions and that there is the right environment for His Kingdom to advance on the earth. So, we are constantly watching and listening, and when appropriate, taking action.

God continues to make His interest known through a number of ways. He wants us to know what He intends to do, when and where He intends to do something, and what role He expects us to play in it. He will do nothing on earth before revealing it to His prophets. He will do nothing on earth except through us. So, what are we really looking for? We are looking for His interest, His timing, and the role He expects us to play in protecting and carrying out His interest. Throughout the Old Testament, the New Testament, and even today, God continues to speak through:

- Prophetic utterances

- His Word, which contains many promises—some that might have already been fulfilled and others that are still to be fulfilled

- Dreams and visions

- An audible voice, at times

- An impression in our spirits for us to know His intentions, at times

130

• Situations around us

We must watch for the fulfillment of prophetic words and for His promises. When God has spoken a word or made a promise, we must stand on the promises to see them come to pass. This means that we should go into the courts of heaven, reminding God of His promises and asking for justice.

The author in Isaiah 62 understood that God had promised to restore Jerusalem and to make her a praise in the earth. This speaks of His intention for Jerusalem. The author therefore in verse 1 boldly states that: *"For Zion's sake I will not hold my peace, and for Jerusalem's sake I will not rest, until..."* The author was holding God to His promises until it was established. In verse 7 of this same chapter, again the watchmen are to hold their stand on the promises of God until God brings fulfillment to His promises to establish Jerusalem. As Kingdom agents, we must be aware of His promises and intentions, and we must watch and enter into the courts of heaven, presenting our case until we see fulfilment.

Whereas the good watchman is aware of God's promises, Isaiah 54 describes the bad watchman as being ignorant. Ignorance speaks of being uninformed, lacking knowledge and understanding. This also includes having information but not knowing what to do with that information. As Kingdom agents, it is imperative that we have understanding of developments within Kingdom Security.

We must be knowledgeable of matters of the Kingdom of God. We must be able to operate in and from the realms of the spirit. We must be watching for physical manifestations that have spiritual implications. If we fall short here, Isaiah 54 describes us as ignorant. How many ignorant watchmen are standing watch today, who are simply missing the mark or are ineffective because of ignorance? They lack information in the physical and the spiritual realms. They are ignorant of God's promises and intentions.

Many believers are not spending enough time in the Word of God. The Word of God allows us to know biblical promises and principles. Bad watchmen lack scriptural knowledge and are therefore unable to apply the Word of God to situations. Good watchmen know how to stand on biblical principles and God's promises. Bad watchmen are unable to rightly divide the Word of truth.

God is calling for the Kingdom sentinels to arise and to be rightly positioned.

Good Watchmen Are Not Silent; Bad Watchmen Are Dumb Dogs

Good watchmen are vocal and are good communicators. Isaiah 62 describes the good watchman as being vocal—not silent. There is a tendency sometimes when we look at a situation, to hold a position on it but not speak up concerning the matter. A good watchman understands the power of words, that life and death lie in the power of the tongue. We must be vocal and speak up on matters of truth. We must release sounds into the atmosphere that affect the realm of the spirit.

- Interceding and petitioning

- Decreeing and declaring

- Verbally coming in agreement with

- Verbally opposing

Not being silent also speaks of taking a stance or holding a position on a matter. There is a saying that comes to mind: "Silence gives consent." When we remain silent on matters that we should take a stand against, or we don't clearly act on our position, it is as if we are giving consent to that agenda of darkness. It calls for a position to be taken. It calls for action; otherwise, it can be considered as being silent on a Kingdom matter and by virtue of such, condoning or consenting to the agenda of darkness.

The book of Esther gives us an example of how the agenda of God was being opposed by the agenda of darkness. God's interest was to preserve the Jews and to bring them back from captivity after seventy years. The particular agenda of darkness at that time was to annihilate the Jews. These are opposing agendas. Mordecai portrays the Kingdom watchman throughout the text in a very compelling way. He was rightly positioned. He sat within the king's gate. Mordecai intercepted the plot against the kingdom. But take note of the fact that he didn't remain silent. He took a position, and he took action by reporting to the queen, who in turn reported to the king.

Mordecai continued to remain watchful and became aware of the decree that was signed to annihilate the Jews. He immediately chose not to remain silent but moved into action instead. He fasted and prayed. He even moved his prayer and fasting to stand before the king's gate. His message to Queen Esther was also very profound. He challenged her not to remain silent lest deliverance would come from elsewhere. He urged her to take a stand against the ungodly agenda and to rise and take action.

There is much that we can learn from Mordecai and Esther today. One can question the position of the church as it relates to ungodly legislation. Is the church silent, and by virtue of such consenting to ungodly legislation that is being passed? We have seen several ungodly pieces of legislation passed in the last few years. As a result, the clergy is being threatened to offer services that can be opposing to biblical truth. In some cases, threats of subpoena were made to have sermons censored. This is a time when we must be sober and vigilant according to 1 Peter 5:2. We must stand at the gates of our communities, our nations, and our governments. Satan, through these ungodly pieces of legislation, is seeking to usurp the authority of the church and to make us ineffective in our Kingdom administration.

Are the watchmen rightfully positioned in the King's gate to intercept and to cause ungodly legislation to be aborted? Remember, the watchmen must be proactive. We must intercept the plan and cause it to be aborted before it becomes legislation. We must not be silent about it. As Kingdom agents, we must become mobilized; we must take a stand. We are not powerless. Like Queen Esther, we can cause the reversal or the overturning of ungodly legislation.

In Isaiah 56, the watchman is described as a dumb dog. This in itself is paradoxical. A watchdog is meant to bark, to growl, and to alert its master of the impending danger of an intruder. What good is a watchdog that cannot bark? It is useless for security purposes and has disqualified itself from such a task. Even so, the watchman who cannot alert or does not alert anyone of impending danger to the Kingdom of God is useless.

Kingdom agents must be able to take authoritative positions and actions in defense of Kingdom Interest. Kingdom agents must be effective communicators. We must know when to speak and when to be silent. We must know whom to speak to and what to say. If not, we have disqualified ourselves and can be considered as a dumb dog.

Good Watchmen Are Persistent; Bad Watchmen Are Sleeping, Lying Down, and Loving to Slumber

Persistence is key to accomplishing tasks. As we study the watchmen described in Isaiah 62, they are persistent. They were prepared to not hold their peace day or night. They would not be easily deterred, even if it seemed like nothing had happened. Sometimes, when we are watching in prayer over certain situations, it seems as if the exact opposite of what we are praying for is happening. In times like these, discouragement can set in, or we may feel ready to give up and throw in the towel. The sentinel is stouthearted and persistent. He knows his God and is confident that He is well able to bring it to pass. He is prepared to give God no rest until he sees the establishment of Kingdom Interest.

Isaiah 56 describes the watchmen as sleeping, lying down, and loving to slumber. They are lethargic. It is understood that one cannot watch from such a position. A lethargic watchman is a prayerless watchman. A prayerless watchman cannot hear God and is therefore not in tune with Kingdom Interest. He is unaware of the advances of darkness throughout the earth.

Let us take a moment to focus our attention on prayerlessness. We can find ourselves in a state of prayerlessness and be absolutely unaware of it. Mosy and Chinyere Madugba, in their book *Understanding the Ministry of the Apostolic Woman,* discussed the matter of prayerlessness and have pointed out some conditions that will help us to identify when we are in a state of prayerlessness. They pointed out that prayerlessness can simply be defined as being in a state of not finding joy in prayer. [15]

Prayerlessness goes beyond not praying at all, but it also encompasses not praying as one ought to or not praying as one

135

is led to pray. When one prays at one's convenience, or maintains an inconsistent prayer life, this is also prayerlessness. If we are not careful, prayerlessness creeps in easily, and we will quickly become like the sleeping dog described in Isaiah 56, loving to slumber.

Prayerlessness is not the only matter of concern here for this watchman. This watchman loves to slumber. He is more concerned with his own comfort, leisure, and pleasure than he is with Kingdom Interest. He is therefore useless as a watchman.

Good Watchmen Are Busy with Kingdom Intentions; Bad Watchmen Are Greedy Dogs

The Isaiah 62 watchman is certainly busy with Kingdom Interest and executing Kingdom Security. He knows how to access the courts of heaven and present his case for Jerusalem. He is petitioning God to establish according to His promises and to make Jerusalem a praise in the earth.

Isaiah 56 describes the bad watchman as greedy. He is preoccupied with his own satisfaction and never has enough. His drive for self-gratification keeps him distracted as a watchman and operating with a broken focus.

Good Watchmen Understand God's Timing and Seasons; Bad Watchmen Have Selfish Ambitions and Lack Kingdom Initiatives

Understanding of God's timing and seasons is important in Kingdom Security. Remember, we must understand what it is that God intends to do and when He intends for it to be done. Kingdom Security must work with God's calendar. An excellent example of a Kingdom agent who understood God's timing was Daniel. Daniel understood from the books that Jeremiah had prophesied that after seventy years, the desolation of Jerusalem would have been completed (Daniel 9:1–2). As a Kingdom agent, Daniel entered the courts of heaven to petition and remind God of His intention. He repented on behalf of the people. We must know when God wants something done, and we must be prepared to give birth to it.

Isaiah 56, on the other hand, describes the bad watchman as having selfish ambitions and lacking Kingdom initiatives. He is busy building his own agenda and building his own kingdom. Kingdom Interest is not his priority. As believers, we can so easily become caught up in building our own lives that we can lose track of why we are here on earth.

Having examined the benchmarks as discussed in Isaiah 56 and 62, we must assess ourselves as Kingdom agents. Where are we? A good watchman or a bad watchman? This is a call to wake up Kingdom agents worldwide so that we will stand effectively in our towers and on our walls to execute Kingdom Security. If you have found yourself with any traits of the Isaiah 56 watchman, then it is time to wake up and make the necessary adjustments. I clearly heard the Lord saying that "they think that they are watching, but they are sleeping. Go and wake My people from their slumber."

Efforts must be made to transition cross over from the watchman described in Isaiah 56 to become the watchman described in Isaiah 62. Here are some things that we can do:

1. Overcome prayerlessness and spend more time in

the Word and in prayer. In so doing, we will become knowledgeable of Kingdom Interest.

2. Make Kingdom Interest our priority.

3. Multitask as you keep your spirit engaged with Kingdom matters continually.

4. Don't be a deaf dog. Train your ears to hear God and understand what it is that He is saying.

5. Don't be a blind dog. Train your eyes to see in the realms of the spirit.

6. Don't be a dumb dog. Communicate with God. Ask questions about what you see and hear in the Spirit. Be vocal. Decree and declare, announce, etc.

7. Learn to access the courts of heaven and petition God for justice.

Regardless what sphere of influence in which we are called to operate, we must remain watchful in the spirit and in the natural. We must watch from the widest spectrum possible. It is time for the Kingdom sentinels to arise in full strength and align themselves in Kingdom Security.

——————— ••••• ———————

8.

———◆———

Let the Kingdom
Sentinels Arise

*For though walk in the flesh, we do not war according to
the flesh. For the weapons of our warfare are not carnal
but mighty in God for the pulling down of strongholds.
Casting down arguments and every high thing that ex-
alts itself against the knowledge of God, bringing every
thought into captivity to the obedience of Christ.*

2 Corinthians 10:3–5

Operating from the Spirit Realm

As His Kingdom government, our primary place of administration is in the spirit realm. We must understand that a lot of
what we are dealing with is conceived in the spirit realm and
then birthed or made to manifest into the earth realm. Also, our
prayers and declarations cause changes in the spirit realms that
yield results in the earth realm. Therefore, it is imperative that
we understand the spirit realms and how they operate, that we
come into the understanding of the protocols and rules of en-
gagements in the spirit realms as His Kingdom Government.

Many believers are stuck by operating from the earth realm and are often still limited in operating from the spirit realms. To be most effective as kingdom administrators, we must understand the realms and become comfortable accessing the spirit realms. I remember the Lord telling me at one point that I must learn how to navigate in the spirit realm. I did not have much understanding at that time of what it all meant. I started to pursue a deeper understanding of the spirit realms. And as I continued to yield myself to God in time and fellowship, I started to gain a greater understanding of the spirit realms. God wants us to come into greater understanding of the spirit realms. Take a moment and pray this simple but profound prayer right now:

My heavenly Father, I pray that the eyes of my understanding will become enlightened right now; that I may come into deeper understanding of the operation of the spirit realms, in Jesus' name, amen.

There are so many possibilities and activities taking place in the spirit realm daily that we need to be a part of. He wants us to be comfortable in maneuvering and administrating from that position. What is needed is the discipline and the diligence to build our spirit man to the extent that it will help us to access the spirit realms more easily.

Where we sometimes struggle to pursue the understanding of the spirit realms, workers of darkness are making great sacrifices to understand the realms so that they can be most effective and dominate there. Encountering God in the spirit realms is not limited to a chosen few. We are all spirit beings and have access to the spirit world. That is where we encounter God as well. He is Spirit, and it is through our spirit that we encounter Him.

Whether we are aware of it or not, our spirit is engaged in the spirit world daily. However, we must make it purposeful. That is where we administrate on His behalf as Kingdom agents. When we assume our positions as Kingdom sentinels, we can watch within the spirit realms and administrate on behalf of heaven. We must understand the awesome authority and responsibility that we have within the spirit realms. This is necessary for the effective execution of Kingdom Security in this season.

Evil is being inspired from dark sources within the spirit realm and then birthed in the earth realm, especially in matters relating to ungodly legislation and with the emerging global and sociocultural trends. We must continue to work at safeguarding Kingdom Interest and allowing God to birth His agenda on the earth in its appropriate season. It is important that we continue to push toward biblical values being embraced and upheld by society.

If we are to examine developments as it relates to a genderless society, we will see that the stage is by far already set for its implementation. Processes have been meticulously worked out and are now being implemented. Curricula have already been developed with an inclusive approach in all subject areas. Even though this is still being resisted in many countries, there are countries that have moved forward to implement SOGI 123 and similar programs as part of their curriculum.

Children are being taught that gender is fluid and are encouraged to explore their sexuality. According to this type of teaching, children have the right to determine what gender they would like to embrace. Our concern in Kingdom Security is that such a notion directly opposes God's Word, which teaches that we were created male and female. Gender is determined by God while we are in the womb and is then ac-

141

knowledged at birth. This is not a matter of choice. We must be able to treat everyone with respect and dignity despite their sexual orientation. However, our concern remains, as believers, our ability to stand as scripturally correct and to be able to uphold biblical values without becoming homophobic. Whereas we do not condone the sin, we must love all of God's creation and treat them with dignity and respect.

As we continue to look at the steady move toward a genderless society, we also find that some teachers' training programs are now also preparing teachers to teach in a genderless classroom. Parent and family support groups are already in place to stand with parents whose children may have decided to change their gender. They help parents to embrace their child's "choice of sexuality" and encourage society to embrace gender fluidity as well. Media platforms are lobbying and celebrating families with children who have chosen to be a different gender from what they were born. Simply put, the stage is already set, and all key players are already positioned, for a grand entrance of a genderless society.

Should the Body of Christ just roll over and play dead? As we examine this from the standpoint of Kingdom Security, we can ask these following three questions:

1. How do we respond to these present developments? What approach can we be taking, and can these trends be reversed?

2. In hindsight, what specific approaches could we have taken to have prevented this from reaching thus far?

3. Moving forward, what proactive approaches in Kingdom Security can we consider to avoid future encroachment on God's Kingdom Interest?

In our attempt to answer these questions, we will take some time to focus on some dimensions of prophetic intercession and its role in Kingdom Security.

Prophetic Intercession

The study of prophetic intercession is a very broad one, but for the purpose of this writing we will just explore some aspects that are most relevant for Kingdom Security. Kingdom Security will lead us to intercede on behalf of communities, governments, and nations. As Kingdom sentinels, we must continue to remain vigilant concerning global developments. In so doing it is imperative that we tap in to God's Kingdom Interest for this season and cause it to prosper in the earth realm, as well as to disrupt satanic interests. Our intercession must therefore be Spirit-led.

Prophetic intercession is fueled by the Holy Spirit, for we on our own cannot know what we ought to pray for. It is the Spirit of God that knows the mind of God and therefore helps us to intercede according to the will of God (Romans 28:26–27). There is only one way to know the heart and mind of God concerning any matter, and that is through the Holy Spirit. So even when we see something in the natural that may need our prayers, we must connect to the Holy Spirit, who will direct our prayers. Because the Spirit of God is all-knowing, it helps us as His agents to become proactive as we intercede over matters, or even as we administrate on His behalf.

Prophetic intercession engaging prophetic dimensions as one is interceding. Let us take a moment to look at five prophetic dimensions and how they can assist us in our intercession.

1. Sight

The first prophetic dimension that we will discuss is the ability to see in the spirit realms. As we study the Bible, we can find where it makes reference to seers. These biblical seers were persons who were able to see in the spirit realms on behalf of others. Prophets are also seers. Watchmen and prophetic intercessors must be able to see into the spirit realms. This can be through:

- Open visions

- Dreams

- Trances

As God allows us to see things in the spirit realms, we are responsible to engage Him about that which we see. We must seek clarity and understanding until it becomes clear. We must also seek out further instructions from Him concerning what was shown to us. The more we engage Him concerning what we are seeing, the more our seeing will develop.

2. Hearing

There are persons who can clearly hear the voice of God. And not only can they hear God, but they can also hear other voices and sounds in the spirit realms. There are times when I have heard a popping sound in my ears, after which I can hear conversations taking place in the spirit realms. This ability to hear in the spirit can also be very useful when we are in the courts of heaven, but it is also necessary to receive instructions from God. We must train our ears to hear God. It is in our time of fellowship with Him that our ears can be trained to hear His voice. Make time to communicate with Him and then to wait on His voice. He is a speaking Father who loves to speak to us, but we are often not available to listen. Train your ears to listen and to hear His voice.

3. Sensing/discerning

There are times when you might just get a sensing in your spirit about something. You may not be quite able to put your hands on where it is coming from, but you just have a strong sensing. This is one of the ways that God speaks to us. With that sensing often comes a burden for prayer and intercession. Go before God concerning the things that you are sensing and allow Him to shed light on the matter and give you further instructions for intercession.

4. Coming into knowledge of

The Spirit of God can reveal information to us in many ways. We can find ourselves coming into the knowledge of things that we could not have known on our own, but only through the Holy Spirit of God. Like the gift of the word of knowledge when it is in operation, this can include the use of sight, hearing, and even sensing. This can often happen when we are in deep intercession. God will give us knowledge of certain things that we could not have known on our own. It is for a matter of prayer.

145

5. Traveling in time, places, and realms

It can be common when in intercession, that as you press in the spirit, you can find yourself in another location. This can be spiritual or physical locations. There are intercessors who have found themselves in the spirit in another geographic location on a prayer assignment. Others have found themselves in legislation halls. Prayer assignments can take you several places in the spirit realms. There are also times when intercessors find themselves in heavenly realms where they encounter angels and other spirit beings

We were released with gifting grace and abilities. The apostle Paul admonishes us to seek out the best giftings of the Spirit. For us to be most effective in prophetic intercession, we must seek to develop the grace and the giftings that are on our lives. Do not take them for granted. The more that we can flow in these prophetic dimensions, the more effective our intercession will become. Develop your spiritual senses. Know what giftings you flow in and pay the price to develop in them. Bring it before God and have Him increase it. You can also read books or attend seminars that teach on the gifts of the Spirit. Take it to the next level and do not be contented with where you are at. The more you engage with that gift, the more it will develop. Press in and talk to God about what you are seeing and hearing. Take time to inquire and question Him.

The Two-Pronged Approach

As we read the book of Nehemiah, we find an excellent approach on how a sentinel can use prophetic intercession in his execution of Kingdom Security. Nehemiah's approach was also proactive. He engaged Kingdom Interest, and at the same time, he was ready to disrupt satanic interest. He was aware that Kingdom Interest was to rebuild the wall around Jerusalem, which he was determined to see accomplished. He also knew that the satanic interest was to prevent the walls of Jerusalem from being rebuilt, and he was prepared to deal with that, as well. It is important that we operate in this same manner. Nehemiah positioned his men to work on the wall, but at the same time they were well prepared and equipped to deal with the encroachment of satanic interest.

As we examine God's instructions to Jeremiah (1:10), we find that God also outlined this same approach to this prophet. As a prophet to the nations, Jeremiah was instructed to root out and to destroy, but also to plant and to build. "To root out and to plant" points to satanic interest, while "to plant and to build" points to Kingdom Interest. Together they form an approach in prophetic intercession that is necessary for Kingdom Security.

To effectively practice Kingdom Security, we must therefore work with a two-pronged approach, as Nehemiah did and as Jeremiah was instructed to do. Jeremiah was instructed to root out, to pull down, and to destroy, but also to plant and to build. We must be birthing Kingdom Interest in the earth realm. Simultaneously, we must be aborting satanic interest before it can be birthed in the physical realm. Let us examine these two processes and how we can implement them as we practice Kingdom Security.

Birthing Kingdom Intentions

It is an amazing season to be alive. There are many great and awesome things that God wants to do on earth, and He is waiting on you and me to partner with Him. What an incredible honor. Destiny scrolls are waiting to be birthed into the earth realm—destiny scrolls for individuals, ministries, communities, governments, and nations. The birthing process of Kingdom intentions into the earth realms takes place through three stages, namely, the conception stage, the incubation stage, and the birthing stage.

Prophetic intercession is key throughout all three stages. We all have spiritual wombs with the capacity to receive deposits through the Spirit of God that allow us to conceive and give birth to His intentions in the earth realm. During the conception stage, we must position ourselves and become intimate with Him so that He can deposit thoughts, ideas, strategies, burdens for prayer, and more into us.

One of the misconceptions that exists is that we can only become intimate with God through worship, prayer, and reading the Word. Intimacy with God takes place anytime and anywhere we avail ourselves that He can deposit His will and thoughts into our spiritual wombs. This can also take place when we are watching in the spirit or even when we are watching in the natural. The key is to be connected to the Holy Spirit so that we can become impregnated. The inquisitive nature of the watchman also creates an opportunity for impregnation. Again, whether you are inquiring in the natural or in the spirit, it creates an opportunity to become intimate and impregnated with heaven's thoughts. So, as we are searching out matters concerning current global developments and sociocultural trends, these must also be seen as moments of intimacy with God and therefore opportunities to become impregnated, as well.

Intimacy with God becomes possible through prophetic dimensions, where we are allowed to see and understand by the Spirit, hear and understand by the Spirit, sense by the Spirit, and come into knowledge of things that we could not have known unless by His Spirit.

Once we have become impregnated with the intentions of God, we must allow it to incubate and mature to the fullness of time. This is what we consider stage two in this process. During this stage, we must be praying through that which is deposited into our spiritual wombs. This may include praying for persons, processes, and systems that are involved. It can also include monitoring things in the natural and in the spirit. During the incubation stage, we must stay abreast with that matter as a hen will sit on her eggs until the full time for them to hatch has come.

It is also during the incubation stage that we prophesy and declare the will of God concerning the matter. We must speak and declare forth the intended outcome. As Kingdom administrators, we must envision the necessary processes for that matter and legislate it in the realms accordingly.

We might never know how long the incubation period will last. What we do know is that we must persist in using whatever strategy that has been given us to use until we get to the place of birthing. Birthing is the final stage. In this stage, we see the manifestation of that which was deposited in our spiritual wombs coming to pass. We need to birth heaven's plans from the spirit realms into the earth realm. God wants us to lay hold of His intention for every predestined season and cause them to be birthed in the earth realm.

We cannot become so preoccupied with satanic interest that we overlook the importance of birth of God's intentions in the earth realm. Kingdom Security concerns itself with both.

Disrupting Satanic Interest

Jesus told a parable in Matthew 13:25 of a sower who went out to sow while the enemy sowed tares among the wheat.

Another parable put He forth unto them, saying, The kingdom of heaven is likened unto a man which sowed good seed in his field: But while men slept, the enemy came and sowed tares among the wheat, and went his way.

—Matthew 13:24–25

This scripture helps us to understand how satanic interest manages to penetrate in its attempt to disrupt God's agenda for earth and for humanity. The good seeds can be seen as God's Kingdom Interest. The parable tells us that the tares are sown while men sleep. That is a major red flag in Kingdom Security. As we examine this parable, we can conclude that someone was not alert, was not watching, or was not stationed; simply put, someone was asleep. So, when we do not fully understand our role as sentinels or we are in a slumbering mode, the enemy will find opportunity to come in and to make evil deposits in the midst of what God is doing.

The tares sown in the vineyard can be seen as evil deposits or satanic interest. If we can prevent these evil deposits from being made, then there will be no need to root out that which was sown. When we miss that opportunity and they grow among the wheat, then it becomes more difficult to deal with. Jesus told the disciples that to uproot them at that stage can also cause damage to the wheat. Therefore, it is always more complicated for us to deal with ungodly systems and legislations once they are already put in place. Prophetic intercession helps us to remain watchful and proactive to prevent the enemy from carrying out his own agenda or attempting to interfere with God's agenda.

The following graph will help us to understand how satanic interest is deposited into evil wombs and birthed into the earth realm. It will also help us to understand our role in causing the abortion of evil deposits and in destroying evil wombs.

Satanic interest, including ungodly legislation, does not happen overnight. These things also go through stages. They are first conceived in the hearts or minds of individuals. For the purpose of this writing, we will consider these to be "evil wombs." The enemy is looking for evil wombs where satanic deposits can be securely nurtured and eventually birthed into the physical realm. They may start with an idea or be as simple as a desire. This is the first stage, and it is what we will call the conception stage. It is at this stage that a satanic deposit is made in an evil womb.

When individuals or groups begin to conceptualize and

plan out that thought or idea and build support around it, then it moves into the second phase, which is called the incubation phase. This stage includes everything that takes place with that thought, desire, or idea from the point of its conception to the point that it is ready to be carried out. Everything that is necessary for its success is carefully and methodically thought out, consulted, and put into place. During this stage, much planning and processing take place. Many awareness campaigns take place during the incubation phase.

The last stage is the birthing stage. That is when the thought has been incubated in its evil womb to full maturity, and it is now ready to be executed. It is now already in the legislative halls. Support groups are rallying for its enforcement. Acts of terror are being carried out.

Understanding and visualizing this process is important for Kingdom Security. We too often tackle the problem at the birthing stage, where we are faced with much resistance. Kingdom Security and prophetic intercession at its best **MUST** be able to catch this process at the conception stage and trigger an abortion of the satanic interest. Not only must we cause an abortion of the evil deposit, but we must also identify the evil wombs and destroy them.

It is important that the evil wombs be destroyed as part of the destruction process. Any evil womb that is allowed to survive will conceive again.

How does one identify evil wombs? An evil womb can be an individual, a group, a culture, or even an organized system, government, or institution that is open for evil deposits. How do you destroy them? Pray that they disintegrate or are otherwise destroyed. We must speak barrenness to those wombs, causing the evil womb to become incapacitated; causing them to dry up;

causing them to shut down; causing evil wombs to no longer accept evil seed but only be available for godly deposit. Kingdom Security calls the sentinels and Kingdom intelligence to operate from this level.

This book is calling on the Body of Christ to position itself to execute Kingdom Security. As we examine global developments and sociocultural trends, we find that there is an urgency to shift into this level of security, where we are dealing with matters at the conception stage. The prophet Elisha intercepted the king's evil plan to attack Israel at the conception stage and triggered an abortion by alerting the king of Israel of those evil plans. It is time to operate in the prophetic dimensions with precision. We must make every possible effort to avoid it from progressing to stage two, for it is much easier to deal with it at the conception stage than at the incubation stage.

However, if we have missed the opportunity to deal with it at the conception stage, we will still have the opportunity to deal with it in the incubation stage. At this stage, it will be a bit more complicated, as there are more processes that are already underway. At this stage, we must be thorough in uprooting and shutting down every process and plan that might already be in place or in any developmental stage. Dealing with it at the conception stage or the incubation stage means that we are still proactively involved in the process.

What we really want to avoid at any cost is to find ourselves dealing with satanic interests after the birthing stage. It is already there and is therefore far more difficult to deal with. Many economic, sociocultural, political, and governmental structures have been formed this way. Marxism, communism, the holocaust, terrorism, segregation, occultism, and many others satanic interests all began as a thought in someone's mind, but then they were given the time to incubate and then be birthed into legal and governmental structures.

If there is ever a time for Kingdom agents to be positioned, it is now. As we examine this present time, we will find that there is an accelerated intrusion of satanic interest in the earth realm. Christian values continue to be challenged, and biblical truths are being thrown to the ground. There has been so much that has already been put in place to support satanic interest and demonic structures. Signs of the end times are blaring.

However, I believe that we are approaching a time of a great spiritual awakening upon the earth. Once again God will pour out His Spirit, especially in places that have been closed to the gospel, for creation is awaiting the manifestation of the sons of God. We must be relevant to the times and the season in which we are living. We must come into the understanding of Kingdom Security and stand our watch. There are Kingdom intentions to be birthed and satanic interests to be crushed. Let us position ourselves today in Kingdom Security and let all Kingdom sentinels arise.

_____ ..... _____

APPENDIX

The Language of the Watchman

Language must be appropriate for the assignment. There are times when we are seeking and petitioning, and the language must reflect that. There are times when you will be positioned to decree and declare. There are times when prophetic utterance will be necessary. Other times, this might call for militant language.

Confront	Break evil assignment
Disturb	Cause to be reversed
Disrupt	Cause to be aborted
Frustrate	Cause to be exposed
Uproot	Cause to come to pass
Pull down	Intervene
Destroy	Speak death to evil plans
Condemn	Remove limitations
Push back	Decree
Give birth to	Declare

Cause to come forth	Build
Annihilate	Plant
Cause to be aborted	Set in place/order
Diminish	Shift
Bring to nothing	Bring alignment
Renounce	Come in agreement with
Render powerless	Thy Kingdom come
Break evil influence	Your purposes superimpose
Scatter	

BIBLIOGRAPHY

Alves, Elizabeth. *Becoming a Prayer Warrior*. Minneapolis, MN: Chosen Books, 2016.

Bradshaw, Gordon E. *Authority for Assignment.* Lakebay, WA: Kingdom House Publishing, 2011.

Bradshaw, Gordon E. *I See Thrones!* Lakebay, WA: Kingdom House Publishing, 2015.

Brewton, James. *From Footmen to Horsemen*. Lakebay: Kingdom House Publishing, 2016.

Clayton, Ian. Realms of the Kingdom Volume 1. UK: Sons Of Thunder Publications Ltd, 2016

Clayton, Ian. Realms of the Kingdom Volume Two. UK.: Sons Of Thunder Publications Ltd, 2016

Cook, Bruce et al. *Aligning with the Apostolic*, Vols. 1–5. Lakebay, WA: Kingdom House Publishing, 2013.

Cook, Bruce. *The Eighth Mountain*. Lakebay, WA: Kingdom House Publishing, 2017.

Femrite, Tommy. *Invading the Seven Mountains with Inter-*

cession: How to Reclaim Society through prayers. Lake Mary, FL : Creation House, 2011.

Guyon, Jeanne. *Experiencing God through Prayer*. PA: Whitaker House, 1984.

Henderson, Robert. *Operating in the Courts of Heaven*. Midlothian, TX: Robert Henderson Ministries, 2014.

Henderson, Robert. *Unlocking Destinies from the Courts of Heaven*. Midlothian, TX: Robert Henderson Ministries, 2016.

Ighama, Nosa. *The Authority of the Name of Jesus*. Open Gate Ventures, 2012.

Kauffman, Mark E. *The Presence-Driven Leader*. USA

Madugba, Mosey & Chinyere, *Understanding the Ministry of Apostolic Women*. Nigeria: Spiritual Life Outreach Publications, 2010.

Neuhaus III, John. *Melchizedek in Our Midst*. USA, R&R Printing, 2016.

Pearcey, Nancy. *Total Truth*. Wheaton, IL: Crossway, 2008.

Ramirez, John. *Unmasking the Devil*. Shippensburg, PA. Destiny Image Publishers, 2015.

Sheets, Dutch. *Watchman Prayer*. Minneapolis, MN: Bethany House, 2000.

Trimm, Cindy. *When Kingdoms Clash*. Lake Mary, FL: Charisma House, 2007.

Vincent, Ricardo. *Understanding Dreams and Visions*. USA, 2013.

Wagner, C. Peter. *Spiritual Warfare Strategy*. Shippensburg, PA: Destiny Image Publishing, 2002.

Wagner, C. Peter. *Territorial Spirits*. Shippensburg, PA: Destiny Image Publishing, 2012.

END NOTES

1. Nancy Pearcey, Total Truth (Wheaton, IL: Crossway, 2008).

2. John Neuhaus III, Melchizedek in Our Midst (R&R Printing, 2016), 140.

3. Robert Henderson, Operating in the Courts of Heaven (Midlothian, TX: Robert Henderson Ministries, 2014).

4. Ian Clayton. Realms of the Kingdom, Volume Two: Trading in the Heavens (UK: Sons Of Thunder Publications, 2016).

5. Ian Clayton, Realms of the Kingdom, Volume 2.

6. Bruce Cook, The Eighth Mountain (Lakebay, WA: Kingdom House Publishing, 2017), 158.

7. Tommi Femrite, Invading the Seven Mountains of Intercession (Lake Mary, FL : Creation House, 2011), 19.

8. Ibid., 8.

9. Ibid.

10. Mosey & Chinyere Madugba, Understanding the Ministry of Apostolic Women (Nigeria: Spiritual Life Outreach Publications, 2010), 199.

11. Ibid., 64.

12. Ibid., 132.

13. Ibid., 66.

14. Ibid., 177.

15. Ibid., 125.

CPSIA information can be obtained
at www.ICGtesting.com
Printed in the USA
BVHW042111120121
597696BV00017B/474

9 781647 733520